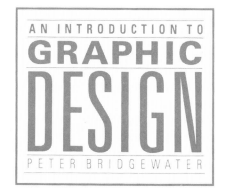

AN INTRODUCTION TO

GRAPHIC
DESIGN

PETER BRIDGEWATER

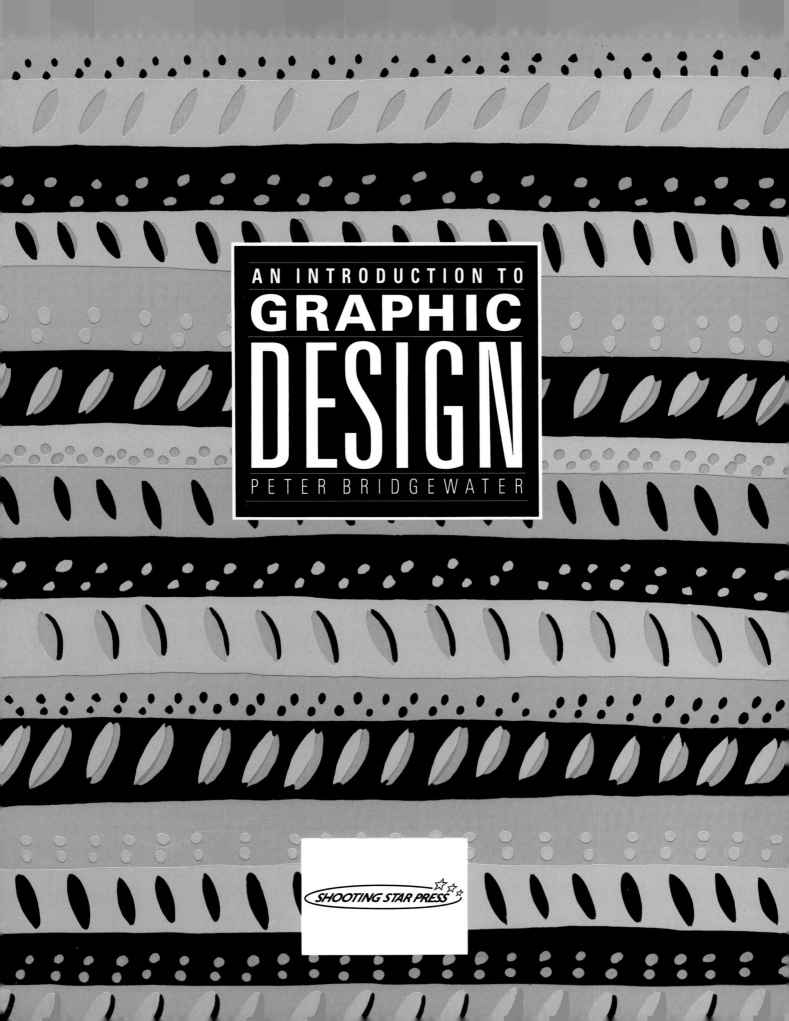

AN INTRODUCTION TO
GRAPHIC
DESIGN

PETER BRIDGEWATER

SHOOTING STAR PRESS

A QUANTUM BOOK

Published by Shooting Star Press, Inc.
230 Fifth Avenue, Suite 1212
New York, NY 10001
USA

ISBN 1-57335-463-5

This book was produced by
Quantum Books Ltd
6 Blundell Street
London N7 9BH

ART DIRECTOR: PETER BRIDGEWATER
EDITOR: CLARE PUMFREY
PHOTOGRAPHER: LARRY BRAY

Typeset in Great Britain by
Central Southern Typesetters, Eastbourne
Manufactured in Hong Kong by Regent Publishing Services Limited
Printed in Singapore by Star Standard Industries Pte. Ltd.

Picture credits

Key to abbreviations:

a = above, b = below, c = centre, l = left, r = right.

Agfa-Gevaert/Artworker **54/55**; Bridgeman Art Library, **13**; Larry
Bray **83l**; Caterpillar Inc., **15ac**; Chrysalis Visual Programming **91l**;
Computer Animator/Bruce Carter, **115**; Crabtree & Evelyn/Tessa
Traegar **89a, 98l**; Daily Telegraph Colour Library, **16ac bc**; Design
Council, **14/15, 15bc**; ET Archive, **11r**; Freemans, **10a, 11a**;
Lorraine Harrison **83r**; Ashley Hunt **18bl**; Marshall Editions, **87**;
The Moving Picture Company/Electronic Paintbox, **91r**; Robert Opie
Collection, **12, 16bl**; Pavilion Books/Guy Rycart, **89b**; Photo Images,
82; Petersburgh Press Ltd, **19br**; Rob Shone **78/79**; Snark **16br,
17al**; Tate Gallery/© SPADEM **16al, 18br**; Vienna-Akademie der
Bildenden Künste, **17r**; Zoffany: Reproduced by gracious
permission of Her Majesty the Queen, **17b**.

CONTENTS

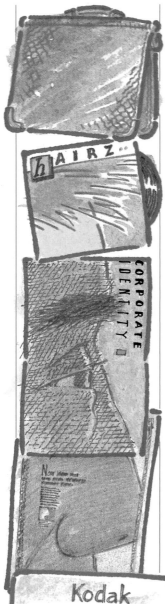

ACKNOWLEDGEMENTS

I would like to thank the following designers for contributing their work to *'Design Portfolio'*:

Simon Balley
Balley Design Associates/Oval Motors

Chris Bigg
Salute

Lawrence Edwards
Skylife

Bob English
English Markell Pockett/Equinox

Pat Gavin
London Weekend Television/The South Bank Show

Steven Horse
Chrysalis Records/The Fountainhead

Terry Jeavons
Jeavons Lander Associates Ltd./Alto

Bernard Lodge
The Moving Picture Co/Barclays Home Mortgage

Victor Loke
Doyle Dane Bernbach Advertising/Metro

Peter Windett
Peter Windett & Associates/Crabtree & Evelyn

Nick Clark
Qdos/Tristar

I would also like to thank Ed Carr (RT Partners), Annie Ellis and Lorraine Harrison for their illustration work and Larry Bray for his photography. All those mentioned gave generously of their time.
I am also grateful to Graham Bell and 'Artworker' for supplying materials and equipment and to Nick Law for his editorial help.

INTRODUCTION

This book is directed towards students and those of you who are new to the graphics industry. It is intended as a practical book to help you understand design techniques, procedures and the design industry itself, so that when you are commissioned to do a piece of commercial work you will understand some of the language and appear more confident and capable of tackling the work.

I have tried to make this book visually exciting, and at the same time communicate the information effectively. This is the essence of successful graphic design. As the reader, you will judge this book, just as the client and customer will judge your work. Commercial design is basically a service which is bought and sold, so your design must satisfy the client, the audience and your own design standards. To win clients you have to be good, and to keep them you have to be consistent, professional and reliable.

As an employer of designers, I am aware that many design graduates are neither technically nor mentally prepared for commercial work. They are unable to come into a studio and deal with even the most basic of tasks. This widely held view can make finding work difficult; it can also result in exploitation. To avoid such problems you must appreciate the skills which employers demand, so that you are aware of the aesthetic issues involved in design and have the ability to *produce* your ideas within the practical constraints of deadlines, budgets and clients' needs.

This book introduces you to graphics, gives you a realistic flavour of the work and helps you handle a job professionally. There are other excellent specialist books which cover areas such as typography or printing procedures in greater detail. For those of you trying to decide which direction to take after college, I have given a brief description of the design areas in which you can be employed and how you go about winning work. For the designer who decides to freelance, I have included advice on how to set up and run a small business, with a checklist of do's and don'ts.

Graphic design is an exciting and competitive industry. If you are to succeed, you must develop a businesslike approach and not feel personally attacked if you lose a commission or end up having to compromise your ideas. Try to be positive in such situations – sometimes clients know better and a job is more successful as a result of their contributions. Remember, taste is subjective and so the design solution you decide on may not always suit your client or employer.

Your experiences, talent and ambitions will be different from mine, and you will develop your own methods of working, but I hope, nonetheless, that some of the tips and short-cuts I have learnt, and pitfalls I have avoided during my years working as a graphic designer will be helpful to you. Keep your eyes open and try to learn as much as possible from those around you and put it to good use. Graphics is hard work and highly pressurized, but it is also a fantastic way of earning a living. I am still thrilled when I deliver a visual which is met with enthusiasm, or I see the colour proof of a job for the first time and it looks good. These moments of satisfaction make up for the hassle and late nights spent finishing a job, and are the reasons why I keep doing it.

P. G. Bridgewater

PETER BRIDGEWATER

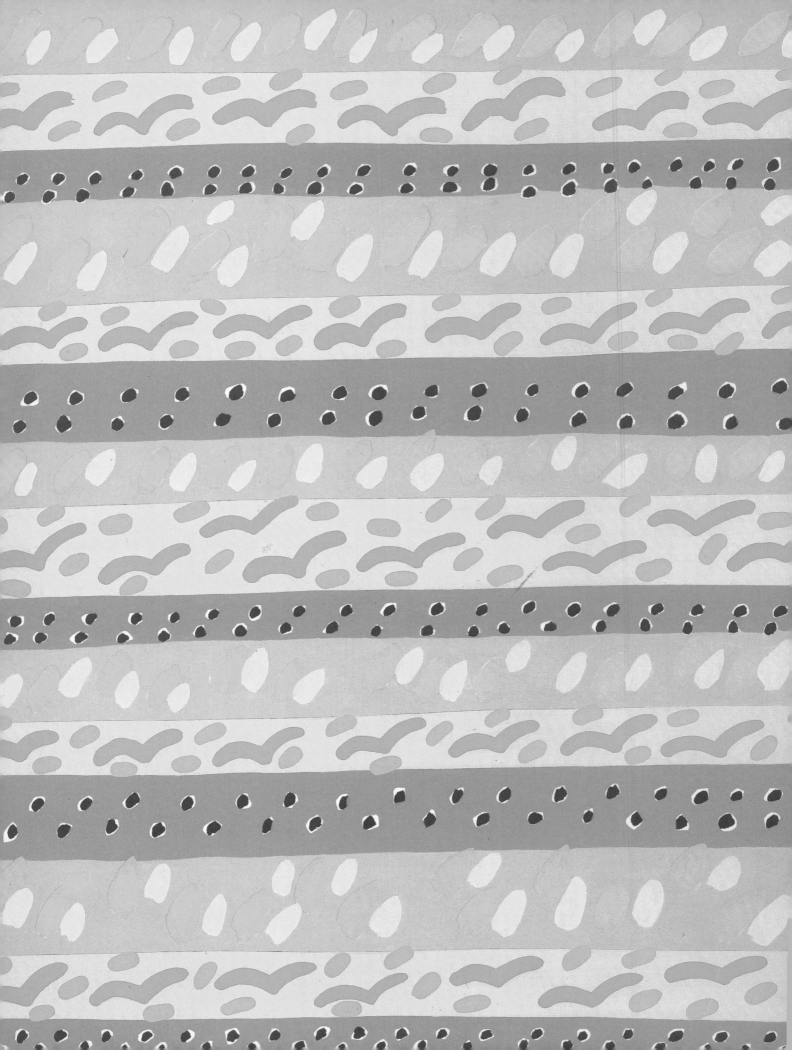

CHAPTER ONE

FUNDAMENTALS

The aim of a graphic designer is to communicate a message to his audience successfully through the organization of words and images. The graphic designer Paul Rand defined the designer as being 'like a juggler, demonstrating his skills by manipulating various ingredients in a given space'. This is an apt description although it does not give adequate credit to the aesthetic judgements involved. The principle, however, remains basically the same whether applied to the design of a letterhead or the creation of computer-generated television images. A well-designed poster or book may appear to be the result of almost casual effort on the part of the designer. This is rarely the case. More often it is the result of a lengthy process, including experimenting with many options until a satisfactory one is found.

Good design has to take into consideration the practical constraints imposed by a client's brief – the budget, schedule and audience. The designer acts as a go-between, carrying a message from client to customer. To do this well, a designer must be familiar with all forms of graphic reproduction, and able to work with printers, photographers, illustrators and other technicians.

HISTORY

Throughout its history graphic design has influenced and been influenced by trends in fashion, film, music, history, politics, painting, religion and nostalgia. Early graphic design was produced by craftsmen who were members of trades guilds of printers and signwriters. Many of the first designers employed in television to produce captions trained originally as ticket writers and signwriters. There was no graphic design profession. One man carried out every task required in the production of a book – editing, typefounding, printing, publishing and selling. Graphic design in its modern sense began with printing and the amalgamation of artistic and mechanical elements. It was in the mid-16th century that type design was separated from printing by Claude Garamond and Jacob Sabon. The earliest illustrations were

OPPOSITE ABOVE Albrecht Dürer, Canon cut from *Opus Speciale Misarum.* Dürer's woodcuts are early examples of very strong graphic images.

OPPOSITE LEFT Guttenberg's Bible, *c* 1455, was the first book to be commercially mass-produced and ushered in the age of modern printing.

ABOVE Hiroshige, *Cat at Window.* Japanese prints derive their strength from the simplicity of composition and subtlety of colour.

LEFT The influence of Victorian pattern and ornament is still evident in contemporary design.

TOP Wood engravings, like this one by Thomas Bewick, were the principal method of recording daily events until the advent of photography.

ABOVE Techniques in stained-glass windows demand a simple approach to colour and composition.

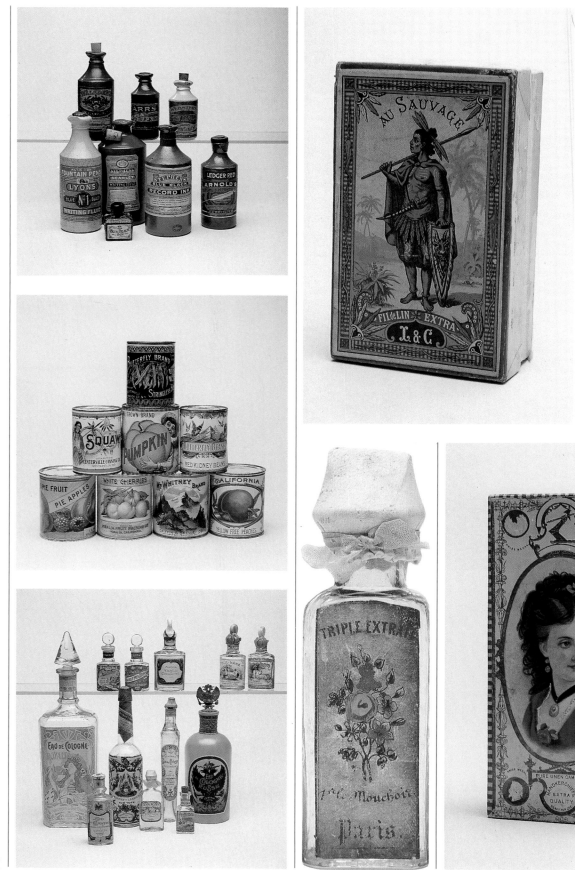

LEFT The packaging industry has always required the three-dimensional application of skilful graphics.

printed from wood blocks, until Gutenberg introduced metal blocks in the mid-15th century.

The 19th century saw printing technology surge forward, after centuries during which little progress was made. By the middle of the century, graphic design had spread into the fields of packaging, presentation, display and advertising, and was established as a profession in its own right. Graphic design continued to develop alongside new ideas and techniques in architecture, industry, engineering, technology and commerce.

Henri de Toulouse-Lautrec (1864–1901) had great influence on the modern medium of the poster. He understood posters as a means of communicating with other people and collecting an audience. He saw the importance of translating his work into print, and took advantage of the developments in large-scale lithography. The classical tradition of centred typography, using various letterforms, had its origins in lettering and calligraphy, but there were innovators who were prepared to challenge existing values in the search for a more effective and original means of communication. Painters such as Whistler and Pissarro designed title pages for books using asymmetric arrangements of type, which broke with accepted standards.

Graphic design today stems largely from the Arts and Crafts movement founded by William Morris (1834–96) in 1884; his ideas were extended to printing and book production as well as furniture, wallpaper and fabrics. In 1890 he founded the Kelmscott Press in an attempt to raise the standard of book design and printing. Morris was a socialist and there was a certain medieval quality in his theory that all products should be created by hand – 'by the people, for the people'.

The next significant influence on design was the decorative arts movement known as Art Nouveau, the name of a shop opened in Paris in 1895. Stylistically its origins lay in Morris's designs. The shapes characteristic of this style are curved and flowing, like waves or flower stalks. It was a graphic style of decoration which was transferred onto a wide variety of objects.

The most important influence on contemporary design, however, was the Bauhaus, established in

TOP AND ABOVE William Morris and other exponents of the Arts and Crafts Movement established a design ethic based on the individual's design skills as a reaction against mass-production.

RIGHT Henri van de Velde, *Tropon.* The Art Nouveau era was a period in which sweeping curves and ornament dominated design.

Germany immediately after the First World War. Walter Gropius (1883–1969), architect, designer and teacher, founded the Bauhaus School of Art and Design in Weimar in 1919. He taught principles which have become fundamental to nearly all aspects of 20th-century design. The philosophy of the school was to bring art and technology closer together. Laszlo Moholy-Nagy (1895–1946), one of the other many gifted teachers at the Bauhaus, said that typography in design should be 'clear communication in its most vivid form'. The Bauhaus created a new typography, and also experimented with printing materials. Herbert Bauer abandoned the use of capital letters in trying to represent sound typographically.

At the same time, the radical Cubist movement was under way in France, led by Pablo Picasso (1881–1973) and Georges Braque (1882–1963).

This freedom from tradition was consolidated in the 1950s by the Swiss designer Jan Tschichold. He advocated simplicity, contrast and primary colours. His asymmetric arrangements of type display exquisite visual judgement. He also combined photographs and type, which was a rare occurrence then. It is no coincidence that Swiss graphic design is still held in high esteem. Switzerland is a country with three official languages, which all appear in most printed literature. The Swiss have had to deal with the problem of order in a rather extreme way.

The role of 'graphic designer' gained real acceptance in the United States, where mass production and mass advertising, together with film, created the need for specialist designers. The idea of producing a corporate image for a company was pioneered by Lester Beall. His design work for Caterpillar led to the use of a company symbol on everything from the earth-moving machines, to the office stationery, and deliberately expressed the essence of Caterpillar's business.

In the last 60 years, the range of typefaces available to a graphic designer has widened enormously. Names of great significance during this period include Eric Gill (1882–1940), artist and typographer, who designed the Gill Sans and Perpetua type families; Stanley Morison (1889–1967), who was a consultant to the Monotype Cor-

14

poration, designed Times and made many other faces available commercially; and Adrian Frutiger who designed the Univers type family in 1957.

Design originally had its roots in printing, and advanced printing technology has influenced attitudes to design. Web-offset printing – that is, lithographic printing on paper which is fed through the printing press from a roll – and computer typesetting, have radically changed the way in which designers work. The designer has always solved problems within the constraints of existing technology, and will continue to do so as technology advances still further with laser printing and computer graphics. New technology merely serves to change or increase the parameters that designers have to work with and will never actually replace the process of design itself.

As the artist used color to create excitement on this page, so can Noreen temporary color help you capture the excitement of beautiful hair. Choose from 14 beautiful shades to brighten or darken your natural color, cover imperfections or blend in unwanted gray.

at cosmetic counters everywhere also professionally applied in beauty salons available in Canada

Noreen

SUPER
COLOR
RINSE

151

CATERPILLAR

LEFT Joost Schmidt's poster for the Bauhaus exhibition, Art and Technology, held in Weimar in 1923. The Bauhaus movement saw radical innovations in all areas of design, including typography.

ABOVE The Caterpillar Inc. logotype, designed by Lester Beall, exemplifies design of company trademarks at its best.

LEFT The aluminium wastepaper bin designed by Walter Gropius shows the influence the Bauhaus had on the design of everyday objects.

ABOVE Herbert Bayer, *Noreen Rinse*, Bayer's asymmetric typography broke the accepted design conventions of his day.

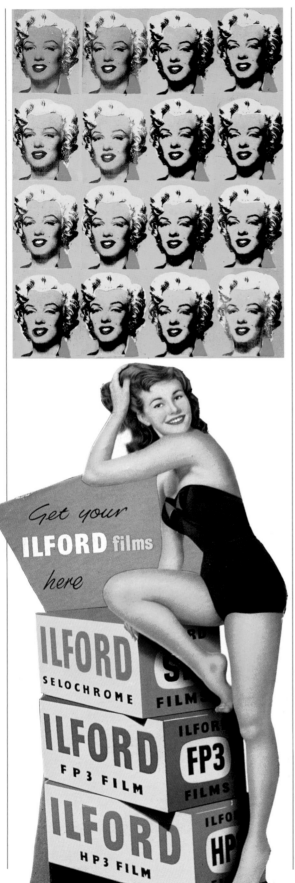

A graphic designer is an orchestrator of words and images. Every designer will deal with typography colour and composition in an individual manner, producing different results. To be a successful graphic designer requires an inherent aesthetic awareness and artistic flair – these are essential qualities. Developing these natural abilities requires practical training. The emphasis now at most colleges is on self-motivation, and, undoubtedly, a period spent exploring ideas and experimenting without the pressure and restrictions imposed by a commercial contract, is invaluable for the development of visual awareness.

Few colleges, therefore, offer the working environment in which students can appreciate why they are learning certain skills. It is difficult to understand the importance of good copyfitting or artwork unless they are put in an appropriate context. The reason for learning how to cast off, or how to mark up copy well, becomes clear very quickly when you begin working. If you are to succeed within this competitive industry, you must be equipped at the outset with a range of basic technical skills and a knowledge of design principles.

TOP LEFT Andy Warhol, *Marilyn Diptych*, 1962. Warhol's striking portraiture typifies the breaking of all conventions in fashion and art that characterized the 1950s.

TOP AND ABOVE London's Carnaby Street reflected the rebellion expressed in pop and psychedelic art that were reactions to the conservatism of art and design in the 1950s (left)

LEFT Students drew from plaster casts of the human figure in order to develop an understanding of anatomy.

ABOVE AND LEFT Life drawing classes are a classic method of developing drawing skills. The ability to draw is important in all design work that involves visuals.

LEFT AND ABOVE Leonardo da Vinci, *Proportions of a Man*. Principles of proportion can be scientifically defined but should never be rigidly applied.

17

DRAWING

All children are encouraged to draw from an early age, but as they grow older, greater emphasis tends to be given to learning the skills of written expression. Consequently, relatively few children develop the skill of drawing more fully.

Drawing enables you to represent your environment or ideas visually on a two-dimensional surface. If you compare this process with the way a graphic designer produces a visual, you can see immediately how useful drawing is. If you can draw, your ability to express an idea is increased. A few well placed lines on a sheet of paper will instantly convey to a client what you are trying to achieve. Many designers, however, feel unable to produce a visual which contains people or objects without having exact photographic references and an enlarger so that they can trace the image. I would be lost without my enlarger, but I advise you to develop your drawing skills. Your visuals will look better as a result; they will have more atmosphere and you may even be able to save yourself some time and money.

A designer should be observant – weak drawing is often the result of not looking properly at the subject. You have to consider composition, proportion and tone. A knowledge of the basic principles of perspective is essential, in order to represent the three-dimensional volume of an object in space on a two-dimensional surface. This knowledge is invaluable, not only for your own visuals, but for assessing the work of illustrators and photographers which you may later commission. Do not be discouraged by the early frustrations you may experience – just keep looking and keep drawing.

Children draw instinctively as a means of expression.

18

PERSPECTIVE VANISHING POINTS

The rules of perspective are applied to show a three-dimensional object on a two-dimensional surface.

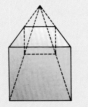

ABOVE In one-point perspective there is only one vanishing point and two sides of the cube are visible.

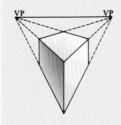

ABOVE In two-point perspective three sides of the cube are visible and two vanishing points exist.

ABOVE In three-point perspective the cube is viewed from a higher or lower point so that three vanishing points appear.

COMPOSITION

When you juggle with areas of text and pictures in a design until the results are visually pleasing, you are 'composing'. You are organizing the type, shapes and colour in such a way that they work well together. The Classical concept of composition was based on a means of dividing up space called The Golden Section. This convention was devised to give artists well balanced points of reference on their paper, from which to work. It is a mathematical method of working out 'ideal' proportions. Similarly, the human figure provides a basis for mathematical proportion – it can be divided up into eight equal sections. Both these concepts are useful but should not be used rigidly.

It is wise to regard systems as servants. Rules of colour, proportion and perspective need only be observed while they serve your purpose; as soon as they impede it, it is your prerogative to change them. To quote Renoir (1841–1919), 'There is much to painting which can't be explained and which is essential. You arrive before nature with theories, and nature throws them to the ground'. Artists and designers now work more intuitively than in the past, but experience and confidence remain the decisive factors affecting composition.

ABOVE Piet Mondrian, *Composition with Red, Yellow and Blue,* 1921.

Mondrian divided space with grid lines and areas of colour aa exercises in composition.

ABOVE Leonardo da Vinci, *Head of St Anne*. The observation of detail is important if you are to develop as an artist.

TOP Leonardo da Vinci, *Perspective Study*. The representation of space was limited to the use of strict geometric rules.

ABOVE Uccello Vase. This study demonstrates the complexities of vanishing points and perspective.

RIGHT David Hockney, *Portrait of Cavafy I*. This portrait has an intuitive quality based on an understanding of classic proportion and perspective.

19

Understanding colour is an integral part of being a designer. It is virtually impossible to be objective about colour because we all use colour in a subjective way. A basic knowledge of colour theory is of course useful, but time spent experimenting with colour is more rewarding. Colour theory shows why it works as it does, but not how to use it to create harmonious or shocking effects, for example. New types of colour, such as dayglo, neon and laser colour, in addition to the natural tones we are familiar with, have had a profound effect on the use of colour in design.

Daylight, or 'white light', is a tiny component of electromagnetic radiation and can be split up into seven different colours, violet, indigo, blue, green, yellow, orange and red – the colours of the spectrum. The colour of an object depends on how much of each of these colours is absorbed or reflected by the surface of that object. The three primary colours are red, yellow and blue. They cannot be mixed from a combination of any other colours, but all other colours can be made up from them. The three secondary colours are made from mixing any two of the primaries together – green (blue and yellow), violet (red and blue) and orange (yellow and red). The shade of a secondary colour will vary depending on the proportions of each primary mixed. Those primary and secondary colours which contrast with each other most strongly are known as complementary colours – orange and blue, yellow and violet, red and green. Complementary colours do not have a common primary colour.

For a designer, working with colour will mean choosing colours which are made up out of the four basic colours used in colour printing. These are yellow, magenta (red), cyan (blue) and black. These four colours can be mixed together in different proportions to achieve nearly all colours. It is important to remember that colour is modified by light. This is particularly important to a designer when specifying colours to a printer. The quality and density of a colour will change if you look at it in two different types of light, so it is best when choosing colours to look at them in daylight.

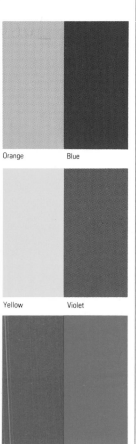

RIGHT White light is made up of red, orange, yellow, green, blue, indigo and violet – the colours of the spectrum. These can be seen when white light passes through a glass prism.

Red

Yellow

Blue

ABOVE The three primary colours are red, yellow and blue and they cannot be mixed from other colours.

Green (blue + yellow)

Violet (red + blue)

Orange (red + yellow)

ABOVE The three secondary colours are green (blue and yellow), violet (red and blue) and orange (red and yellow) and are each made by mixing any two of the primaries together.

Orange | Blue

Yellow | Violet

Red | Green

ABOVE The three sets of complementary colours are orange and blue, yellow and violet, and red and green. These are the colours that contrast with each other the most.

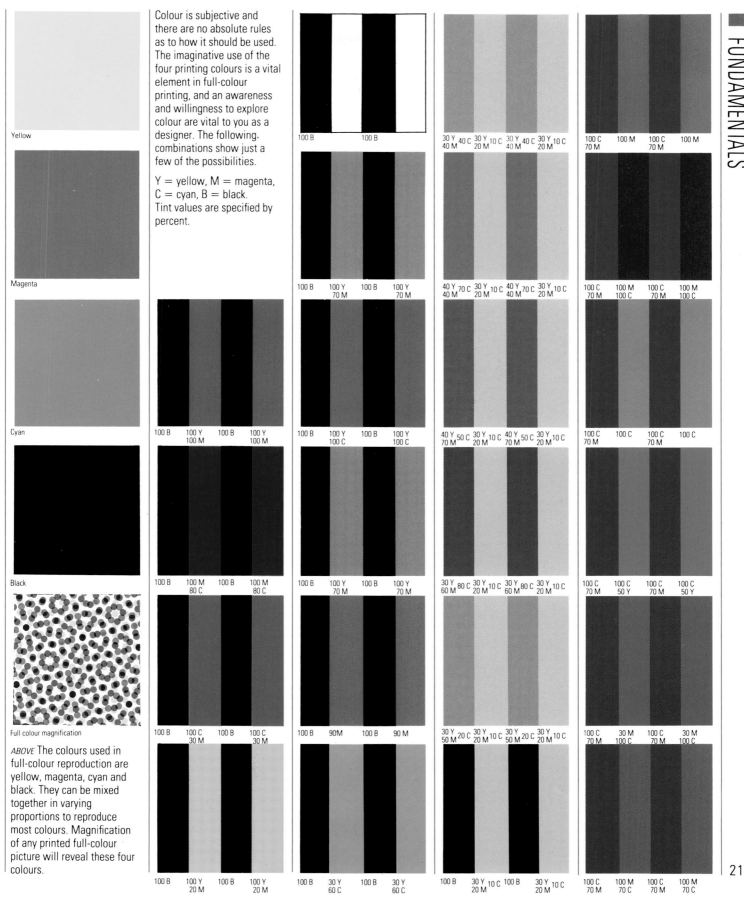

Yellow

Magenta

Cyan

Black

Full colour magnification

Colour is subjective and there are no absolute rules as to how it should be used. The imaginative use of the four printing colours is a vital element in full-colour printing, and an awareness and willingness to explore colour are vital to you as a designer. The following combinations show just a few of the possibilities.

Y = yellow, M = magenta, C = cyan, B = black. Tint values are specified by percent.

ABOVE The colours used in full-colour reproduction are yellow, magenta, cyan and black. They can be mixed together in varying proportions to reproduce most colours. Magnification of any printed full-colour picture will reveal these four colours.

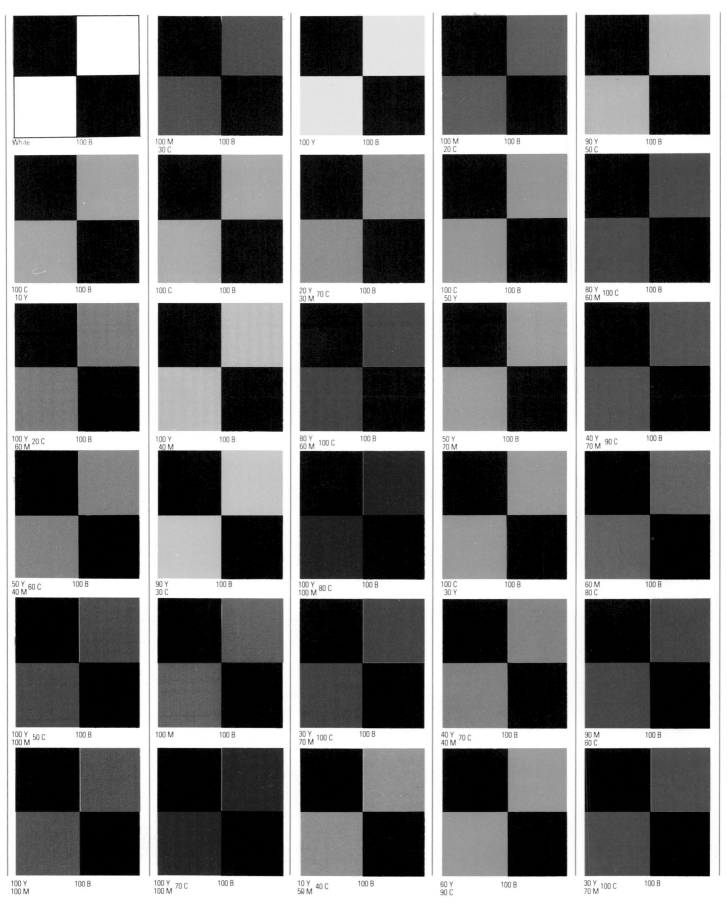

White   100 B

100 M
30 C   100 B

100 Y   100 B

100 M
20 C   100 B

90 Y
50 C   100 B

100 C
10 Y   100 B

100 C   100 B

20 Y
30 M 70 C   100 B

100 C
50 Y   100 B

80 Y 100 C   100 B
60 M

100 Y 20 C   100 B
60 M

100 Y   100 B
40 M

80 Y 100 C   100 B
60 M

50 Y   100 B
70 M

40 Y 90 C   100 B
70 M

50 Y 60 C   100 B
40 M

90 Y   100 B
30 C

100 Y 80 C   100 B
100 M

100 C   100 B
30 Y

60 M   100 B
80 C

100 Y 50 C   100 B
100 M

100 M   100 B

30 Y 100 C   100 B
70 M

40 Y 70 C   100 B
40 M

90 M   100 B
60 C

100 Y   100 B
100 M

100 Y 70 C   100 B
100 M

10 Y 40 C   100 B
50 M

60 Y   100 B
90 C

30 Y 100 C   100 B
70 M

22

Although the colours are identical on these two pages, the check looks totally different on a white base. By replacing the white with black the colours appear much more intense.

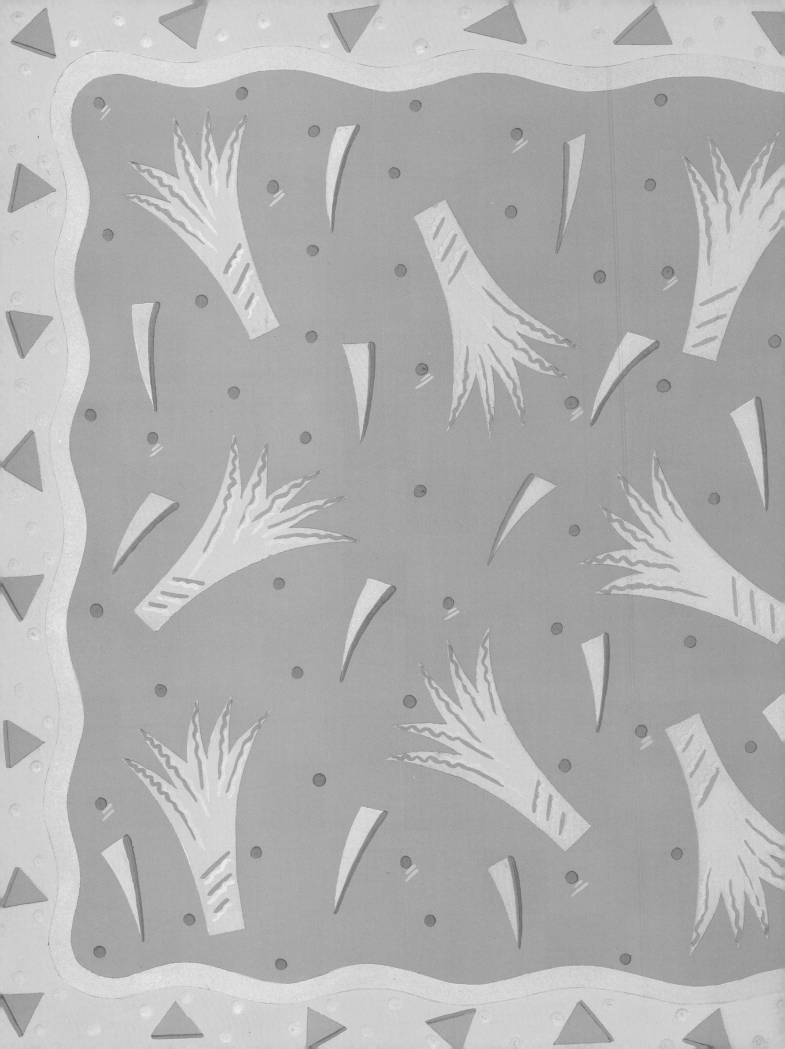

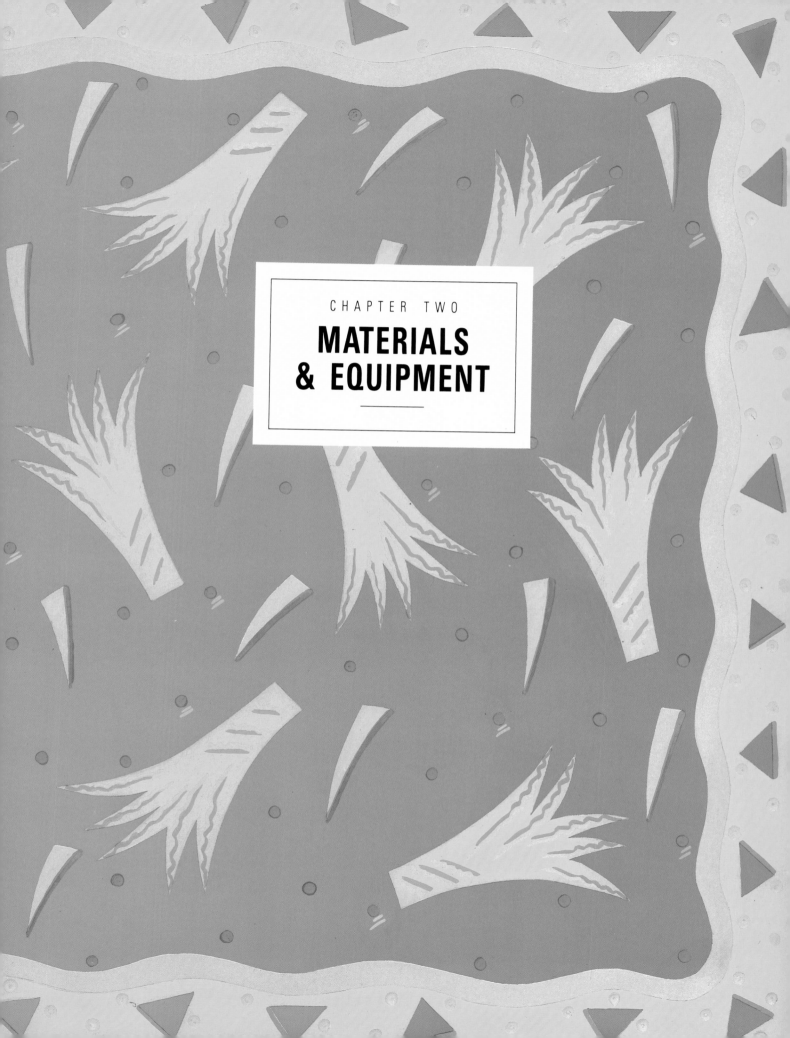

CHAPTER TWO

MATERIALS
& EQUIPMENT

Working to tight schedules and offering a totally reliable service is critical if you are to succeed in the design industry. To do this you must have the right tools. Graphic designers need a comprehensive range of materials and equipment to work quickly and accurately – 'making do' is not cost-effective, nor does it lead to the best work. A good graphics supply company which is either within a few minutes walk or delivers to your door at least once a day is absolutely essential – otherwise you cannot work effectively. Without the back-up of reliable services you will inevitably let clients down. The proximity of such resources should always be one of the deciding factors if you are planning to have a studio.

The initial cost of equipping a studio is considerable, but this expenditure is normally spread out over a period of time. Deciding what to buy will always depend on financial considerations, and before you invest in a major purchase, look

When handling knives, always do so with extreme care. It is particularly easy to inflict serious injuries when changing a blade or using a plastic ruler to cut against. Use the correct implements — a proper metal cutting edge is not very expensive and will last years. Wrap masking tape round old blades before you discard them, so no one else will cut themselves later.

When cutting paper or card, use the correct tool. A lightweight blade used to cut a thick piece of card will result in either a broken blade or damage to the edge you are cutting. This is all common sense, but it is surprising how many accidents occur.

carefully at methods of payment, and whether you can afford it. If necessary take professional advice, but always be sure that you need the item and that it will pay for itself. Try to anticipate your future requirements and think of any labour-saving equipment as an investment. Will you need a larger plan chest (flat file) or PMT camera (stat camera) in a year's time? Are you choosing wisely and can you buy the item secondhand? Should you rent or lease?

If you are working freelance, there will always be items of equipment you would like but may not be able to afford. Once you buy or lease a photocopier which enlarges and reduces, you will wonder how you ever managed without one.

Get into the habit of checking your stock of materials, such as masking tape and adhesive, and have one main order every week to replenish it. To allow yourself to run out of basic materials is both inefficient and unnecessary.

Craft knives *RIGHT* are for cutting heavyweight materials such as cardboard, plastic, hardboard and wood. The handle is shaped for a sure grip and carries spare blades.

Pencil sharpeners *BELOW* are functional but may not give such a sharp point as a scalpel (X-Acto knife) or sanding pad.

Knives *BELOW* which hold a range of interchangeable differently shaped blades are ideal for general studio use.

Swivel knives *LEFT* are designed for cutting curves and complicated shapes in lightweight material such as film or paper. The blade rotates 360° permitting fine control over the direction of cutting.

Retractable knives *RIGHT* with a single blade which can be snapped off and disposed of as it is blunted.

It is wise to keep a good range of coloured papers to hand and order specific colours as and when you need them. Coloured papers and boards are more economical to buy in packs, rather than individually. You should also keep well stocked with tracing and layout pads.

Graphic materials are expensive so try to be as careful and as economical as possible. When using coloured papers, films and boards, don't throw the off-cuts away – there are bound to be occasions when a little scrap of a certain colour will save you the expense and delay of buying a new sheet. Look after the small items of equipment which you use daily, such as ruling pens (technical drawing pens) and set squares (triangles). Keep your technical pens clean and use them regularly, otherwise they become blocked. A generally meticulous approach is one of the most important skills you must acquire. If you work in chaos, it will be reflected in the quality of your work, and you can waste time.

Metal rules *RIGHT* are often used for cutting but are dangerous. A proper metal cutting edge ruler is much heavier and rubber-backed so that it will neither move nor slip.

Cutting mats *BELOW* are either transparent or coloured. The transparent one is for use on a lightbox and the coloured one on a desk. The surface does not break up with use and does not blunt blades. The grid printed on the surface acts as a guide for squaring-up.

Disposable knives *BELOW* are convenient for those unused to changing blades but something of a luxury.

Scissors *BELOW* come in a range of sizes and if looked after will last a considerable time.

Curved blade pocket knife *BELOW* with a protective cap for carrying around in the pocket.

Snapping off blades *RIGHT* requires skill and care.

Scalpels (X-Acto knives) *BELOW* will hold a variety of blades which are all designed for different purposes. Blades can be used for cutting or scraping marks off paper and board, so keep a selection in stock.

Scalpel (X-Acto knife) blades are very dangerous. Wrap masking tape round old blades when disposing of them.

Set squares (triangles) *ABOVE* are essential pieces of equipment in preparing artwork. They come in 45°- and 60°- models and some have bevelled edges for use with ruling pens. This model also has a stainless steel cutting edge.

Ruling (technical drawing) pens *ABOVE* are particularly useful for ruling coloured lines. They take all kinds of ink or paint and the line thickness can be adjusted. Some models are also available with a double head for ruling two parallel lines.

Burnisher *ABOVE* for rubbing down dry transfer. This model takes several differently shaped heads. This one is a 'spoon' tip for working over large areas.

Burnisher *ABOVE* with fixed nylon tip for working with fiddly areas of dry transfer.

Rulers *LEFT* for measuring and ruling lines are precision instruments. They should be kept clean and if they are made of perspex they should not be used for cutting. Their parallel lines are useful for lining up type.

Templates *RIGHT* come in all shapes and sizes and offer a practical way of drawing curves and circles accurately and quickly. They can be placed directly onto artwork and traced round.

Type scales *ABOVE* made of brushed matt metal are easy to read. Buy a model that has point sizes and imperial and metric conversions.

LINEX 1114
DENMARK

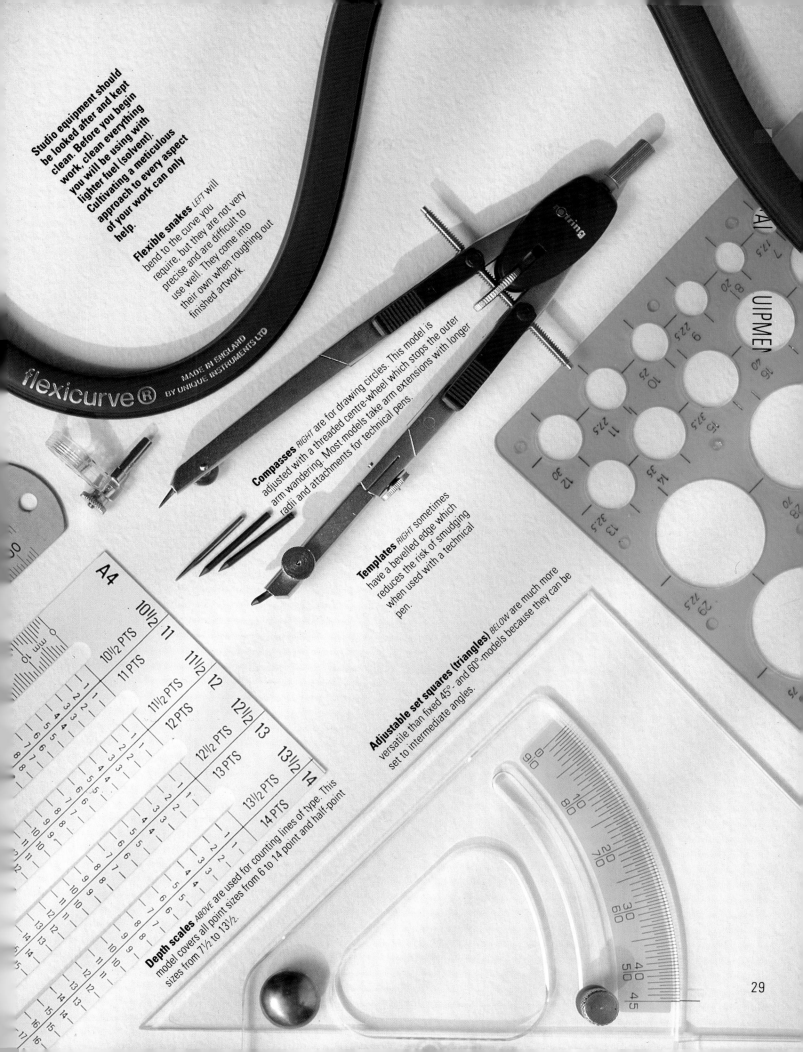

Studio equipment should be looked after and kept clean. Before you begin work, clean everything you will be using with lighter fuel (solvent). Cultivating a meticulous approach to every aspect of your work can only help.

Flexible snakes *LEFT* will bend to the curve you require, but they are not very precise and are difficult to use well. They come into their own when roughing out finished artwork.

Compasses *RIGHT* are for drawing circles. This model is adjusted with a threaded centre-wheel which stops the outer arm wandering. Most models take arm extensions with longer radii and attachments for technical pens.

Templates *RIGHT* sometimes have a bevelled edge which reduces the risk of smudging when used with a technical pen.

Adjustable set squares (triangles) *BELOW* are much more versatile than fixed 45°- and 60°-models because they can be set to intermediate angles.

Depth scales *ABOVE* are used for counting lines of type. This model covers all point sizes from 6 to 14 point and half-point sizes from 7½ to 13½.

Drawing pins *ABOVE*, mapping pins and display pins.

Gummed paper tape *ABOVE* for sealing packages or stretching watercolour paper.

Plastic tape *ABOVE* for strong sealing withstands exposure to sunlight and damp.

Masking tape *ABOVE* is a good all-purpose tape that is easy to lift and re-position.

Double-sided tape *ABOVE* is very secure and not easy to re-position. It is ideal for neat presentation.

Clear tape *ABOVE* — the original general purpose stick tape.

Invisible tape *ABOVE* for neat presentation. Rub the tape down well to make it invisible.

Low-tack invisible tape *ABOVE* is easy to lift and will not damage your surface.

Lithographic tape *ABOVE* photographs as black and is therefore ideal for artwork or stripping up film.

Hand-roller *BELOW* for burnishing down artwork smoothly.

Wax adhesive *RIGHT* enables artwork to be easily re-positioned but will unstick if you place your artwork under hot lights.

Retractable glue-stick *ABOVE* for paper and card.

Waterproof adhesive *ABOVE* for wood, paper, leather and glass. Ideal for model-making.

Blue-tack *BELOW* is useful for fixing photographs and pictures to most surfaces. It is easily removed and can be re-used.

Double-sided sticky pads *BELOW* for display work.

Putty rubbers (erasers)
ABOVE for soft pencil and keeping work surfaces clean.

Eraser *ABOVE* for removing pencil marks.

Eraser *ABOVE* for removing ink on film and paper.

Eraser *ABOVE* for removing pencil marks.

Eraser *ABOVE* for removing overhead projector pen marks from film.

Plastic eraser *BELOW* for removing pencil and dirt without smudges.

Eraser *ABOVE* for removing pencil on drafting film.

Putty rubbers (erasers) *BELOW* can be shaped to a fine point for accuracy.

Eraser *BELOW* for film.

Eraser *ABOVE* for removing ink from tracing paper and drafting film.

Cow-gum rubbers (erasers) *ABOVE* are made by leaving a blob of cow-gum to dry and are very effective in removing excess glue.

Cleaning fluid or lighter fuel (solvent or thinner) *LEFT* removes grease and fingerprints from artwork, cleans instruments and drawing boards, and lifts artwork.

Spray adhesive *BELOW* is quick and easy to use but hangs in the air and the lungs. Spray into an old cardboard box to contain the spread of adhesive.

DRY TRANSFER LETTERING

Dry transfer lettering is lettering which you buy on a plastic sheet and rub down when preparing artwork or mock-ups. There are several major companies producing large ranges of typefaces, as well as rules, borders, symbols and illustration images. Lettering comes in many sizes and some sheets are available in colour. You will gradually build up a collection of sheets which are most usefully stored in alphabetical order. Make sure that they do not get dirty or crumpled.

Dry transfer is applied by rubbing each character down with a soft pencil, or a specially shaped burnisher, once it has been positioned correctly. Rub the letter gently at first until it begins to come away from its plastic sheet – you will see the letter go paler in colour as it is released. Sharp points such as hard pencils will distort the plastic sheet and break up the character. Once the character is released, secure it by burnishing again, but this time with the backing sheet or a piece of tracing paper over the letter to protect it. You can, if you choose, buy a can of protective aerosol spray which prevents the transfer image being scratched or damaged.

All dry transfer is supplied with a protective backing sheet. If you are working on a delicate surface which could mark, leave the backing sheet in position and rub very gently. This will partially pre-release the letter, so that when it is positioned on your work it needs only the slightest pressure to adhere. This backing sheet can also be used for protecting your artwork while applying transfer letters.

If you position a letter wrongly, remove it with a piece of masking or other sticky tape; but do it carefully so as not to damage the surface of your work. If you find the letter is stubborn, a drop of lighter fuel (solvent) will help to lift it more easily. However, don't be too generous, in case the lighter fuel loosens other characters.

Letraset has small horizontal lines under each character which help you to space the letters. If you prefer to space type visually, they are useful for keeping the type straight as you rub it down, or for repairing the edge of a broken character.

Although dry transfer is available in a wide range of typefaces, symbols and other textures designed to speed up artwork, do not always assume it is the answer to every job and use it automatically. Look at other solutions.

1 To pre-release a character, rub gently with a burnisher, holding the sheet in the air or using the backing paper to stop the character coming away.

2 The character is ready to press onto your artwork or presentation once it has gone paler in colour.

3 Place the backing sheet over the character once it is in position and burnish it again to secure it.

Pantone papers enable a printer to match colour as a job is being run. The complete range of 505 papers is available in matt finish and will accept most art media. These colours are also linked into gloss papers and sticky-back film.

Cover papers are mainly used for presentation and display work.

Watercolour papers vary considerably in both weight and texture. All good watercolour papers have a right side that is carefully prepared and coated with size.

Bristol board is a thin smooth card suitable for technical illustration and three-dimensional work.

Watercolour papers often need to be stretched before they are suitable to take the watercolour paint without buckling.

'Not' watercolour paper is the most common paper used for watercolours. The slightly rough surface receives wash and line artwork well.

Hot-pressed papers are hard and smooth and ideal for pencil, pen and ink drawing as well as line and wash.

Cartridge paper is suitable for pencil and early roughs.

Line board takes all types of pen line work without the line feathering. Mistakes can be scratched out with a sharp scalpel (X-Acto knife).

The Pantone colour specifier *LEFT* holds small samples of all the Pantone range on both coated and uncoated papers. **Pantone film colour selector** *RIGHT* for sticky-back film used mainly in presentation work.

PANTONE® 194C

PANTONE® 195C

ANTONE® 207C

PANTONE® 208C

ANTONE® 212C

PANTONE® 209C

PANTONE® 213C

PANTONE® 13C

ANTONE®

PANTONE 321-A
U A

PANTONE 338-A
U A

PANTONE 326-A
U A

PANTONE 339-A
U A

PANTONE 340-A

PANTONE 327-A

Tints available
see Page 40

Marker paper is coated so that the colour from the marker does not bleed through.

Tracing paper is smooth and transparent enough to be seen through, and suitable for fine ink and pencil.

Typo detail paper is used mainly for type roughs and mark-up.

High white layout paper with good resistance to marker bleed.

Layout paper for initial roughs is thin enough to allow type to show through but opaque enough to be drawn onto.

Layout paper

If you are to work effectively as a designer, you must be prepared and able to meet deadlines. Make sure that you have adequate stocks of all the papers and films that you are likely to need.
If you run out of any paper which you use fairly regularly then you are not running your studio efficiently.
Be economical with your materials and save those small off-cuts – there are going to be occasions when a little scrap of a certain colour paper will save you time and money.

Acetate is used for presentation as a clear overlay to keep work clean and for separating artwork.

Drafting film will not stretch or contract, but takes ink and paint. Mistakes can be scraped clean with a scalpel (X-Acto knife) blade.

Clear coated film accepts all studio media.

Photo-opaque film photographs as black. It is a sticky-back film used for masking areas on artwork. It takes pen and ink and is transparent on a lightbox.

Acetate is available in several weights and although it is ideal for presentation, it cracks when creased.

Blue tint drafting film is ideal for colour separated line work.

Soft coloured pencils used for textured colour work. They have a good blending quality and are available in a wide range of colours. You can also buy water-soluble ranges which have more subtle blending possibilities.

Technical drawing pens with ink reservoirs. They give consistent line thickness and are suitable for use on tracing paper, drawing paper and line board. The pens come in a range of line thicknesses and cartridges can be refilled or replaced.

Technical drawing pen with a tungsten carbide tip, suitable for use on drafting film. All technical pens should be held upright to assist the flow of ink.

Drawing inks for technical pens are available in a range of colours and can be thinned down or mixed with one another. The ink is waterproof and smudge-proof when dry and not erasable with a pencil eraser.

Process white and black are particularly useful for artwork which will ultimately be subjected to a photographic process. They are used for cleaning and spotting mistakes or marks and can be intermixed to make a wide range of greys.

WINSOR & NEWTON
PROCESS WHITE
30ml ℮

Refill leads for clutch pencils.

Clutch pencils hold individual replaceable leads and colours and can be retracted come in a range of grades and colours when not in use.

Refill leads for mechanical pencils.

STAEDTLER

782 MARS - TECHNI

Pentel SUPER 0.7mm 2H 12pcs.

SPARE LEAD

Technical drawing pens are ideal for precision ruling and keylining. They must be kept scrupulously clean so that the nibs do not clog up. They have removable nibs and a variety of point sizes can be bought.

Reservoir pen with a square-cut nib for classical calligraphy. This type of art pen can be used with various nibs for lettering and sketching.

Replaceable ink cartridges are cleaner and more convenient to use than a refillable ink reservoir, but more expensive.

PROCESS BLACK

W N

30ml

Absolutely
photograph
blocking po
thin with
lighter tone

MADE IN GT. BRITAIN   REXEL C

MADE IN GT. BRITAIN   REXEL CUMBERLAND De

MADE IN GT. BRITAIN   REXEL CUMBERLAND Derwent Studio

MADE IN GT. BRITAIN   REXEL CUMBERLAND Derwent Studio   Rose Pink 1

MADE IN G

Coloured pencils are popular with illustrators, but can also be used effectively for colour visuals that require subtle colours and tones.

Mechanical pencils hold individual leads that are retractable. A finger push button controls the lead advance very precisely. They are available in various lead widths and are suitable for paper and drafting film.

Drawing pencils are available in a wide range of lead grades which make them suitable for both sketching and precision ruling work.

0,5 mm   Pentel PF3

0,7mm   Pentel PF

0,9mm   Pentel P

STAEDTLER

STAEDTLER MAR

STAEDTLER

GT. BRITAIN

GERMANY

GT. BRITAIN

GERMANY

Magic markers *ABOVE* are spirit-based and will cover large areas of layout paper evenly and without 'lines'.

Hard fibre-tipped pens *ABOVE* are most suitable for addressing packages or simple lettering. Like all spirit-based pens they must be capped when not in use so that they do not dry out.

Pantone markers *BELOW* enable a designer to match colour to the Pantone system of printing inks. This means a colour chosen at concept stage can be accurately reproduced by the printer. The markers are available in 3 nib thicknesses.

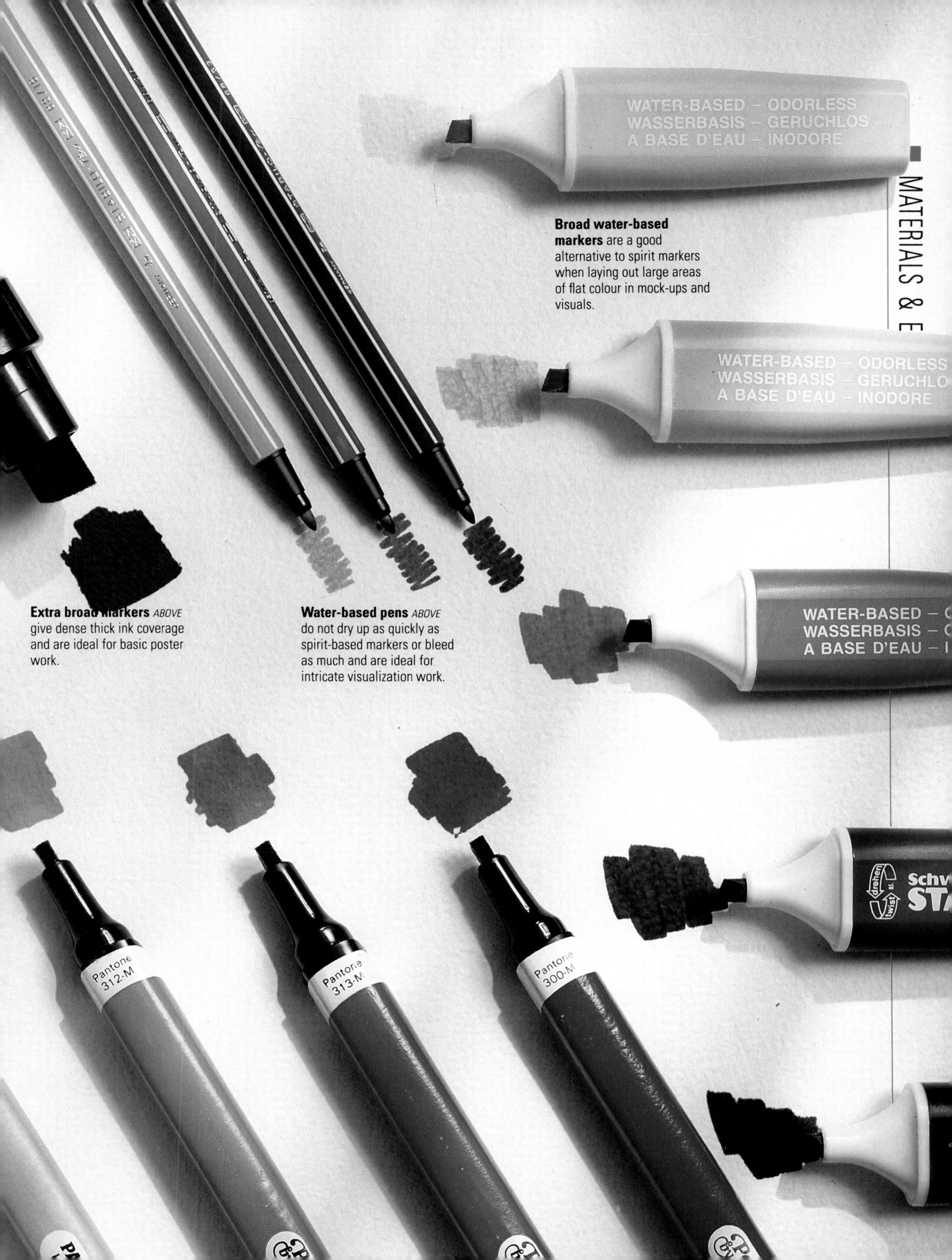

Broad water-based markers are a good alternative to spirit markers when laying out large areas of flat colour in mock-ups and visuals.

WATER-BASED — ODORLESS
WASSERBASIS — GERUCHLOS
A BASE D'EAU — INODORE

WATER-BASED — ODORLESS
WASSERBASIS — GERUCHLO
A BASE D'EAU — INODORE

WATER-BASED — C
WASSERBASIS — C
A BASE D'EAU — I

Extra broad markers *ABOVE* give dense thick ink coverage and are ideal for basic poster work.

Water-based pens *ABOVE* do not dry up as quickly as spirit-based markers or bleed as much and are ideal for intricate visualization work.

Pantone 312-M

Pantone 313-M

Pantone 300-M

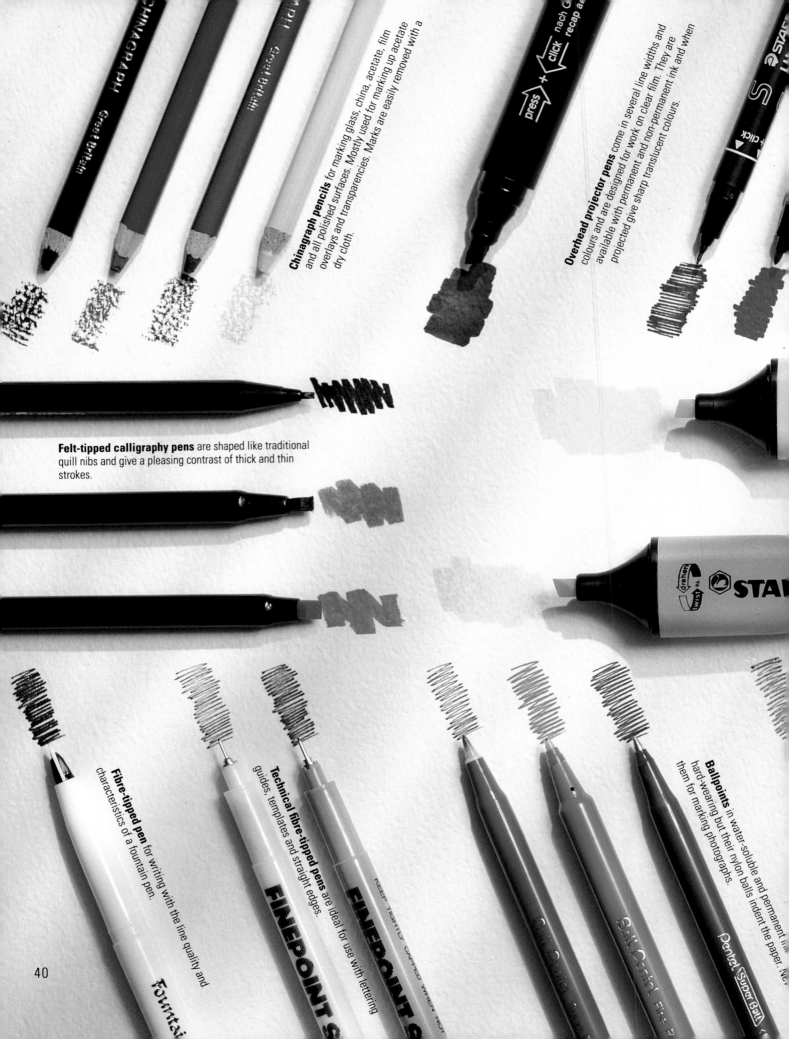

Chinagraph pencils for marking glass, china, acetate, film and all polished surfaces. Mostly used for marking up acetate overlays and transparencies. Marks are easily removed with a dry cloth.

Overhead projector pens come in several line widths and colours and are designed for work on clear film. They are available with permanent and non-permanent inks and when projected give sharp translucent colours.

Felt-tipped calligraphy pens are shaped like traditional quill nibs and give a pleasing contrast of thick and thin strokes.

Fibre-tipped pen for writing with the line quality and characteristics of a fountain pen.

Technical fibre-tipped pens are ideal for use with lettering guides, templates and straight edges.

Ballpoints in water-soluble and permanent ink are hard-wearing but their nylon balls indent the paper, making them for marking photographs.

STAEDTLER LUMOCOLOR

STAEDTLER LUMOCOLOR

LUMOCOLOR · wasserlöslich · wa ... xylotfrei · with

STAEDTLER LUMOCOLOR

STAEDTLER MOTOCOLOR

STAEDTLER LUMOCOLOR

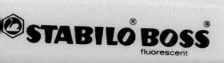

STABILO BOSS ®
fluorescent

Fluorescent markers hold
brilliant water-based colours.
The inks are transparent and
are ideal for highlighting and
emphasizing areas of text.

BOSS ®
fluorescent

PILOT SUPER COLOR
PERMANENT TYPE INK

Metallic gold and silver markers give a good dense
coating of spirit-based ink and will write on almost any
surface.

PILOT GOLD
EXTRA FINE POINT

White markers are useful for ruling in lines or dark
backgrounds when preparing visuals.

Agitese antes de usar ... la presión se
la tinta · poner el tapón después del
edding 78

Traditional ballpoint with dry ink.

Felt-tipped pen which will write on virtually any surface
including glass, metal, plastic, board and wood.

NIKKO name

NIKKO Needlepoi

Fine line pens are ideal for rendering lettering or outlining
areas on visuals before filling in with broader markers.

NIKKO Finepoi

NIKKO Fine

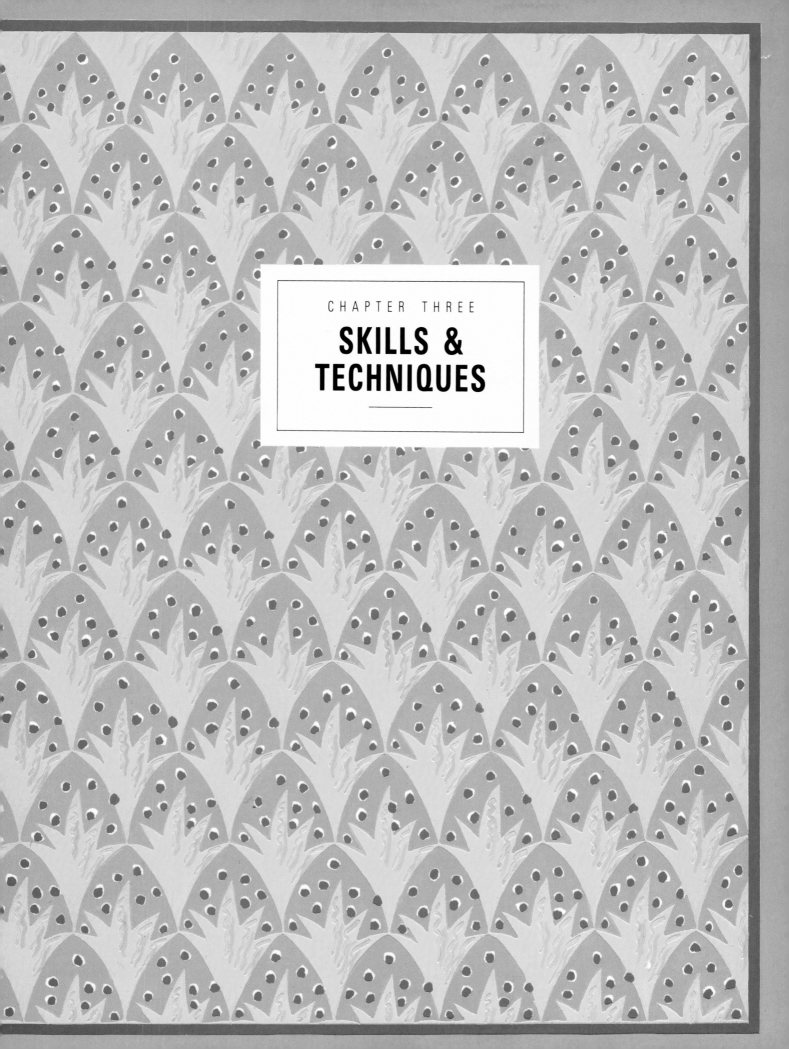

CHAPTER THREE

SKILLS &
TECHNIQUES

airbrush

colour
mark-up

↑ a
gouche

print
preparation

correcting
proofs

visualising

dry
transfer

typography

Producing a visual is an early stage in the process of selling your idea to your client and/or boss. It gives them a good idea of what the finished product will look like. Before you begin work on a commission, always ensure that you have fully understood the brief so that you can proceed with confidence. Don't be afraid to phone your client to sort out any point you are unclear about. Always clarify what the client is expecting to see, too. Visuals can be prepared to many different standards, and if you are being paid for producing simple visuals only, you cannot expect to be paid more if you take them to an unnecessarily high finish. You should always be conscious of time and money.

The standard of a visual will often depend on who is going to see it. If you have worked with the client successfully in the past, they will have confidence in you and this will affect what you need to present to them. If the client is new it is perhaps worth spending more time on visuals than you are being paid for, in order to impress them.

Designers are usually required to present up to three alternative design solutions. It can be confusing to present more than this and lead to compromises. For instance, a client may be tempted by various elements in each of your designs and want them combined in some way. This is rarely a satisfactory solution and should be avoided.

A visual can be prepared in any medium you wish and all designers have preferences. However, your essential equipment will be a layout pad, pens and pencils. The first stage is to produce very quick roughs, or 'thumbnails', usually in pencil or felt-tipped pen, to sort out your own thoughts and ideas. It is very easy at this point to become over-involved with one solution, so try to remain open-minded and investigate the problem in as many different ways as you can. The other trap many designers fall into at this point is spending too much time on one solution which is then very difficult to disregard or change. This early design stage is the most creative and most important, so be prepared to spend time in solving all the problems.

1

2

3

4

1 Clarify your brief on paper and plan your pages before beginning any design work.
2 Put all your initial ideas down as quick mini-roughs, or 'thumbnails'.
3 Produce as many design 'thumbnails' as possible before you decide which to take further.
4 Sketch out a provisional layout and start to think in greater detail about colour and type.
5 Picture areas and content can be indicated quickly and efficiently with markers.
6 These early roughs are to help you solve the design problems, not to show your client.
7 The line illustrations of this visual are now drawn in more accurately. The background colour is applied with marker.
8 Visualize illustrations on a separate piece of layout paper and cut them out to achieve sharp edges.

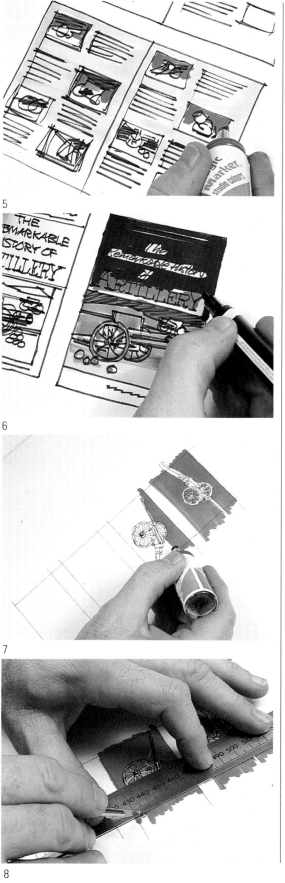

5

6

7

8

Once you have made quick roughs, you should select the ones to take further. Try to remain as impartial as possible. Obviously you will have personal preferences, but always remember that you are trying to provide a solution for a client, not indulging yourself. If your client is visually literate you will be able to discuss these preliminary roughs. Do not show a client roughs in their early stages if they are not used to looking at them – they may cause alarm.

The next stage is to prepare a more finished visual using specific typefaces and images which represent the final printed result. This is the time to think about colour and where and how to place emphasis. A common way of producing colour visuals is with spirit-based markers. They come in a comprehensive range of colours with either broad or fine tips. They have a rather nice quality when used and have maximum effect when used quickly. It does take practice to achieve slick results with these markers and they are expensive. You will discover with experience which media suit you best. Only the main typography should be drawn in with a marker; the text and captions can be indicated with ruled lines or with dry transfer 'dummy' text. If you are using dry transfer text, choose a typeface which resembles the one you would use for the final job. Your graphics technique is very important, and you must develop it. The poor use of markers or badly rendered type will be clearly evident.

The developed visual is now almost ready to present to the client. Show your design off to its best advantage by mounting it onto board with a protective cover. It is common to use black or white mounting board and a dark cover-paper but, of course, you can choose what you like.

Always present work in a clean, professional way to give your client confidence in your ability. Remember to consider what sort of job you are working on. If, for instance, the visual is for a brochure, give the client the opportunity to handle it, page by page, just like a brochure. So, it may not always be appropriate to mount your work flat. If the design requires photographs or illustrations, be prepared to provide examples of the style of work you wish to use.

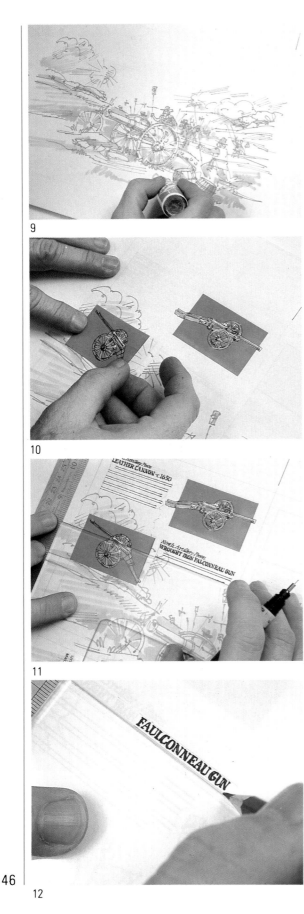

9

10

11

12

The scalpel (X-Acto knife) is used for accurate cutting and is also ideal for handling and positioning small pieces of type.

9 The background colour or design is now rendered in.
10 Mount the separate illustrations onto thin white cartridge before sticking them in position. This will stop any background colour from showing through.
11 Text can be indicated with ruled lines while main headings should be rendered in. Work on a parallel motion or use a ruler and set square (triangle) to ensure accuracy.
12 If you make any mistakes, re-draw the correct version separately.
13 Stick the correction in position over the mistake and cut through both layers with a sharp scalpel (X-Acto knife).
14 Lift up each layer separately and discard the incorrect original. Clean any excess adhesive away with lighter fuel (solvent) and a tissue.
15 Respray the corrected strip with adhesive and position.

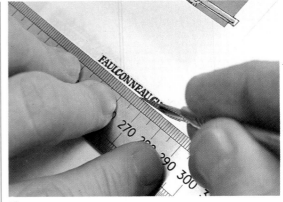

13

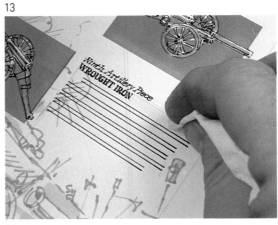

14

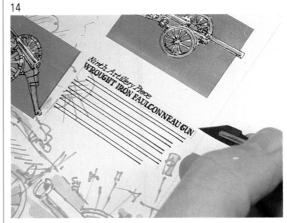

15

16

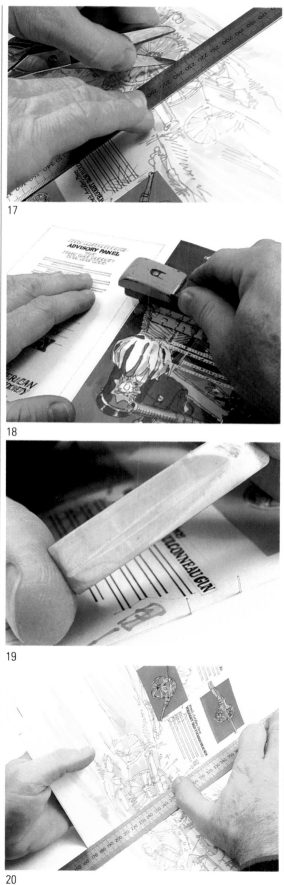

16 Mount your completed visual onto cartridge paper, and trim to size.

17 Score a fold in the trimmed visual using the back of the scissors along a steel rule.

18 When there are more than four pages, staple them together. If the stapler is not wide enough, use it in the open position.

19 A soft rubber (eraser) is ideal for receiving the staple points.

20 Bend the staple ends over with the end of the rule, fold along the score marks and give a final trim, if necessary.

PROTECTIVE OVERLAYS

1 Always use two overlays, a transparent one to carry instructions and an outer paper to protect the work and give it a professional finish. Secure these together.

2 Place the artwork or presentation face down on the transparent sheet. Cut the two top corners of the overlays at 45°.

3 Fold this flap over and secure it to the back of the work with double-sided tape.

4 Trim the excess paper from the other three sides. NB It is dangerous to do this without a steel cutting edge. Stick a compliment slip or label on the cover paper.

1 Keep the markers firmly capped when not in use, otherwise they dry out very quickly.

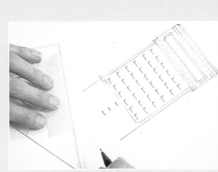

2 Draw the basic outline of your image with a felt-tip pen. Reserve a few dried-up pens for drawing faint lines. A new pen makes a very solid mark.

3 The best results are achieved by working quickly. It is often easier to extend the marker strokes and then cut the finished image out.

4 Test the markers on a scrap of paper if you are using different colours.

5 When using a ruler to guide the line, make sure it is upside down on the paper so that the colour does not bleed underneath.

6 Detail can be added in with finer tipped pens.

7 Highlights can be painted in with white gouache.

8 Detail like this should always be left until last, otherwise the colour from a broad-tipped marker will destroy it.

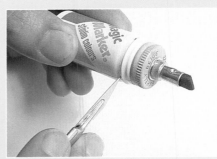

9 If you require a large area of very flat colour, cut the seal round the top of the marker with a scalpel (X-Acto knife).

10 Unscrew the top and remove the wadding. This holds the colour.

11 Hold the wadding side on and employ wide strokes to cover a large area rapidly.

12 The image can now be trimmed and stuck on the background colour.

MAGIC MARKERS

'Magic Marker' is a specific trade name but is often applied generally to spirit-based coloured pens (felt tip marker pens) which are increasingly used in design work. They are available in an enormous range of colours with fine or broad tips, which can be reshaped using a scalpel (X-Acto knife). You can begin by keeping black and a good selection of greys before building up a wider range of colours. Letraset make a range called Pantone Markers and these can be matched directly in colour to a range of inks and papers. As markers are spirit-based, the colour bleeds outwards when they are used. It also bleeds through the paper, so be careful when working that your paper is not resting on anything important.

Their main virtue is that you can cover a large area of layout paper with an even colour, but it does take practice. Make your strokes quickly, otherwise a darker line appears where a fresh stroke of the pen overlaps one that has already dried. To cover a large area quickly, remove the piece of wadding from inside the pen which is soaked in the colour, and use it horizontally with wide sweeping strokes.

If you use a marker with a ruler, remember to clean the edge of the ruler first, otherwise the spirit in the pen will carry the dirt from the ruler on to your layout.

Get into good habits when using these pens, or you will get virtually no use out of them. If you leave markers in the sun or near a radiator they will dry out. Buy a black one and a good selection of greys and then build up the range as the need arises.

> **Design is a fundamental activity based on creativity and innovation. It is imagination put to work to respond to the aspirations and lifestyles of tomorrow's customers.**
>
> RODNEY FITCH 1984

SLICK PRESENTATION

Sometimes a client will want a visual which looks exactly like the final printed job to show his customer. This is quite a straightforward and enjoyable procedure, although daunting if you are doing it for the first time. Remember – the importance of the presentation is the impression it creates. It can be made up of real type and pictures, or mocked up. The better finished a presentation is, the more it will cost; watch your budget.

■ Produce black and white line artwork of all your text matter and any line illustrations. The text can either be typesetting which you have ordered or dry transfer dummy text, depending on whether the 'dummy' needs to be read or not. Real headlines should be used wherever possible, this helps to make the presentation more believable.

■ If the client has not supplied you with real copy to be typeset and you want to use a typeface which is not available in dry transfer, you can always have a random piece of text set and use that.

■ Draw picture areas on your artwork with a fine keyline, and remember to put in trim and fold marks.

■ Having pasted up your artwork, have a bromide or PMT copy (stat) made.

■ Paste in your pictures on the PMT (stat). These can be colour prints you have made or pictures cut out of magazines.

■ Lay the PMT (stat) of your artwork onto a lightbox, and carefully place the pictures over their keylined areas. The black line will be visible through the picture. This is a good method of cropping your pictures to the correct sizes.

■ The assembled presentation can either be mounted flat or stuck into a blank book, or magazine, which a printer will make up for you. This is called a 'bulking dummy' and is used to show the size and thickness of a book or magazine using a specified weight of paper and cover material.

■ If you want a typographic headline in a specific colour, have a dry transfer or 'rub-down' made from your artwork in whatever colour you wish.

■ If you have your flat mock-up copied as a coloured print you will lose slightly on quality, but gain the impression of a finished printed page. Colour xeroxes are less expensive and sometimes of acceptable quality.

■ If you want a glossy or 'laminated' surface, use a clear acetate overlay or a self-adhesive film covering. It is, however, difficult to put this down without creating air bubbles.

The materials are very expensive if you are producing only a single highly-finished presentation. They become more economical if you produce several. This process is very useful for consumer testing – you can simulate a package or book cover which to an untrained eye looks real. The colours on this type of presentation should be accurate. It is advisable to choose colours from a colour matching system so that if the design is approved they can be matched accurately by the printer.

1 Autotype is a process of making dry transfer lettering from artwork and is particularly useful for presentation work.

2 Your artwork is best supplied at the size you want your transfer to be.

3 Autotype enables you to have a transfer made in any colour you specify. Give your supplier a Pantone colour for guidance.

4 Rub the dry transfer down in the normal way.

BOTTOM LEFT Visuals often have to be taken to a highly finished presentation stage. Book jackets, for example, are so important to the success or failure of books that dummies usually have to be prepared to convince clients that an idea is suitable.
By using two L-shaped pieces of cardboard and moving them over the image the most complimentary crop can be found.

ARTWORK

Once your design has been approved by the client, you have to prepare 'camera-ready' artwork, or 'mechanicals', which will be sent to the reproduction house to be proofed. Producing good artwork requires meticulous attention to detail. It is frustrating to look at a printed piece of work which you have designed and see badly spaced typography or a carelessly drawn rule. Errors on artwork which get into print can be disastrous and very expensive to correct.

■ Camera-ready artwork is always prepared flat, in black and white and on line board.

■ Before starting a piece of artwork, make sure that your hands are clean.

■ Fix the line board squarely to your drawing board with masking tape and rule up the areas of your design lightly with a hard pencil or blue pencil. Blue has the advantage of not being picked up on line film when the artwork is photographed during the reproduction process.

■ Your marks must be very accurate, so check all dimensions several times.

■ If your design is very complicated, you can work to a larger scale and then reduce it photographically. As long as your artwork is directly in proportion to its final printed size, you can work to whatever scale you find comfortable. If you work larger, very slight imperfections in the quality of line will be reduced visually as the artwork is reduced.

■ Always keep your equipment and instruments clean. Lighter fuel (solvent) is very good for this. It is also wise to wipe lighter fuel lightly over your ruled-up board with a tissue or piece of absorbent paper to remove the grease and dirt that will inevitably collect there.

■ A soft brush is useful for dusting your artwork. Remember, any imperfections or specks of dirt will be picked up by the camera during colour separation and will, in turn, be reproduced in the printing.

1

2

3

4

T I P

A strip of masking tape on the back of the set square (triangle) or ruler will raise the edge and prevent ink from the technical pen bleeding underneath. It also stops the set square (triangle) from slipping.

1 Rule up the areas of your artwork lightly in pencil as accurately as possible. Always double-check sizes before inking in any lines.
2 When using a technical pen, hold it completely upright so that the lines you draw are of an even consistency. Technical pens are temperamental and have a tendency to dry and clog. Keep them clean and use them regularly.
3 Start by trimming the repro squarely when pasting up typesetting, and it will be much easier to paste up accurately.
4 The positioning of headlines is critical. Although you must check your artwork for mechanical accuracy, the good positioning of large type also requires visual judgement.

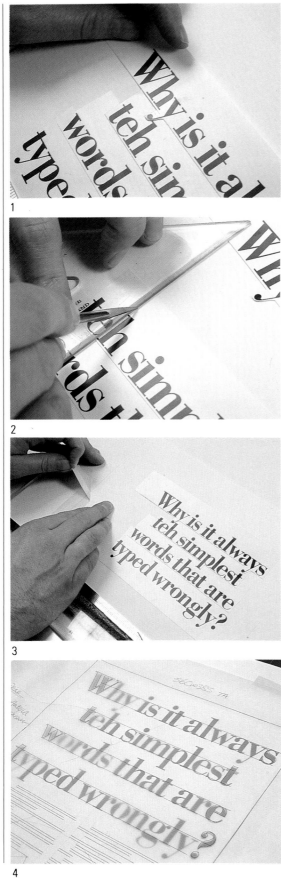

1

2

3

4

You will achieve neat corners by extending both lines further than necessary and scraping them back with a sharp scalpel (X-Acto knife). This takes a steady hand and practice to do well.

1 Descenders of type sometimes have to drop below the cap height of the line beneath in order to look right. Cut around the descender as closely as possible.
2 You may want to adjust the letter spacing of the typesetting. Cut as vertically as possible between the characters and adjust the spacing as required — the vertical cuts will make it easier to re-position.
3 Clean and check the artwork and then have a PMT made. Ensure that the PMT is clean and sharp. Wet any small specks slightly with water and scrape them away gently with a scalpel (X-Acto knife).
4 Position the PMT on the board, place a sheet of tracing paper over the artwork to protect it and give the whole area a final burnish. The overlay can be used to carry instructions for printing.

■ You should always rule in any lines which are to be printed with a technical pen before you begin pasting down typesetting. Once you get adhesive onto the surface of the line board, it is difficult to clean off and will affect the quality of line you draw. Remember to check that your pen is flowing freely before ruling any lines.

■ You can also use tape rules, dry transfer rules (format rules), or rules supplied by your typesetter.

■ Typesetting should be stuck down in position with rubber solution (rubber cement), adhesive sprays or warm wax. They all have advantages and disadvantages, so experiment with all three.

■ Check that text and captions are pasted down in the correct order.

■ Do not discard spare typesetting. You or your client may find last-minute typographic errors.

■ Dry transfer lettering can then be applied directly to the line board, or rubbed down onto a separate piece of paper and stuck down in position on your main board. If you apply dry transfer lettering directly onto artwork, be extra careful not to damage the transfer.

■ You should now clean your artwork again with lighter fuel (solvent) to remove excess glue and dirt. Be careful not to smudge inked rules or disturb dry transfer type.

■ Halftones do not reproduce very well when pasted down as artwork. The size and position of halftones should be clearly marked on the artwork but they should be reproduced separately. All such information and any further instructions should be written on a tracing paper overlay. If you have any doubts about how to present your artwork to a printer or colour reproduction house, call them. It could save you time and money.

■ If you are preparing two-colour artwork, your second colour should be pasted up on a film overlay. This is not always essential because the printer can sometimes separate the two colours on film, but it will be more expensive. Always separate any parts of two-colour artwork onto different overlays which when printed will overlap.

SEPARATED ARTWORK

This artwork is to be reproduced in four colours as shown (bottom right).

The black line work is drawn on the base board and the different areas of colour that are to be made up out of the four process colours — black, magenta, yellow and cyan — are drawn separately on overlays.

An alternative method is to supply only one overlay on which the various colours are indicated; the printer or origination house will then separate these colours at film stage. This method is more time-consuming for the printer and therefore more expensive.

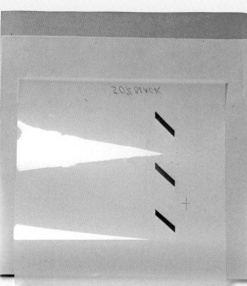

20% BLACK

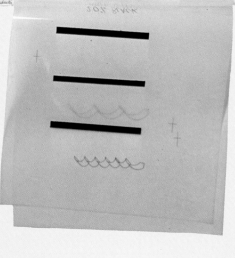

50% YELLOW + 30% MAGENTA

100% BLACK

20% CYAN + 40% YELLOW

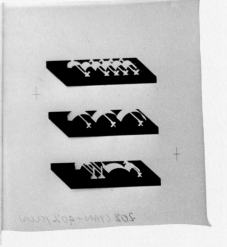

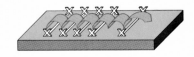

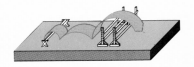

PMTs

PMTs or 'Photomechanical Transfers' (stats) are high quality prints used for the production of artwork. To make PMTs you need a PMT camera (stat camera), special photographic paper and a processor. The machine itself is probably one of the biggest investments a designer will make, but is essential if you need to produce artwork frequently and quickly. You can, of course, have PMTs made by an outside lab, but this can be expensive and time consuming.

The PMT camera is very versatile and can enlarge and reduce, reverse images from black to white, make prints onto clear film, or 'cells', and make screened half-tones. The camera can also be used as an enlarger. Some systems do not even require a darkroom. The most common system uses a positive and negative paper.

When you buy a PMT camera, the supplier will set the camera up, work out an exposure guide for you, and show you how to use it. The paper itself is expensive, so you will learn very quickly. When testing exposures on very fine work, use small strips of paper, not whole sheets. The artwork to be copied is put onto the copyboard, a negative paper is exposed on the image plate, and then contacted through a processor onto a positive paper. The whole process takes only a few minutes.

Main lamps

Lid

Bellows

Control panel

RIGHT The PMT camera must be used in a photographic darkroom because the paper is light-sensitive. Organize the darkroom sensibly and keep masking tape and scissors to hand. You will need the scissors for cutting film and the masking tape for marking the image area on the focusing screen. Keep the darkroom clean, as dust on the copyboard will pick up on the PMT as black specks.

When you buy a PMT camera, your supplier should help you set up correct exposure guides as these will vary, depending on the conditions in the darkroom.

COPYRAPID OFF SET ANODIZED

RPS 2024 COMP

LINE EXPOSURE

The most common use of the PMT camera is to produce copies of line artwork – either the same size, enlarged or reduced – to be used in the preparation of camera-ready artwork. Line artwork, or 'line copy', describes any image that consists solely of black line or areas of black and white, with no shades of grey, or mid-tones. Examples include dry transfer lettering and pen and ink drawings.

Whether you want to copy onto film or paper, the same basic procedure is followed:

■ Switch on the electricity supply to the camera.

■ Switch on the darkroom safe-light.

■ Clean the glass cover to the copyboard and the image plate thoroughly with lighter fuel (solvent), or a special anti-static spray, to remove all greasy fingermarks and dust.

■ Check that your processor is filled with the correct developer.

■ Switch off ordinary room lights so that you are working in 'safe light'.

■ Place your original copy under the glass of the copyboard, ensuring that it is central and squarely positioned.

■ Set your camera to the required size of reproduction: same size = 100%; double size = 200%; half size = 50%, and so on. Some cameras are automatic and some are manual, so the ease with which the desired size is achieved will depend on this.

■ With the lens fully open, check with an eye glass that the image on the focusing screen is sharp.

■ Mark the image area on the focusing screen with pieces of masking tape. This will help you position your negative paper and economize on materials.

■ Set the correct exposure time for your copy on the camera's timer and 'stop down' the lens to the required amount. You will have an established exposure scale which will give you all this information.

■ Turn off the camera's constant light.

■ Place the negative material on the image plate with the light sensitive emulsion side facing the glass, and close the vacuum top. Activate the vacuum, and wait for the desired pressure to be reached.

■ Switch on the main lamps and wait for them to go off at the pre-set time. After exposure, open the vacuum top, remove the negative, contact it with the positive receiver paper, or film, and feed them through the processor. Wait for the recommended contact time. The result should be a clean sharp copy of the original. Complete the procedure by washing and drying the print.

■ If the results are not satisfactory, check your developing fluid and lens aperture or f-stop. Problems are often due to the paper being faulty in the first place, or the paper not contacting properly as it passes through the processor.

■ The negative paper is light sensitive, so must never be exposed to daylight. *Never open packs of light sensitive paper or film except in safe-light, otherwise you will spoil the entire pack.*

Negative carrier/focusing

Main lamps

Lens

Copyboard

Backlight

SCALING ILLUSTRATIONS

Before an illustration can be sent for origination, it must be clearly marked-up with instructions which indicate what size the reproduction should be, what area of the picture is to be used and which areas of the image are to be cut out. This procedure is known as scaling.

There are several ways of doing this, but the most accurate method is to draw a traced keyline of your original at the size required onto a tracing overlay fixed to your artwork in position. This keyline enables the printer to size the image exactly. You can enlarge or reduce your illustration on an enlarger. If it is a transparency, project it through a slide projector onto a flat wall, then trace it onto your overlay. Specific instructions can be written on this overlay and the original attached to the artwork. Always treat originals with care. Put transparencies and prints into protective bags or envelopes, to prevent damage.

Another method of scaling an illustration is to fit a transparent overlay onto your slide, or picture, and indicate on the overlay the area to be reproduced. You should write the dimensions of the finished image on the overlay and cross-hatch the area not required. If you are working on a photograph never use a ballpoint pen to do this. The pen will make an indent through the overlay and damage the original.

If you are required to give the size of the finished image as a percentage of the original – half of the original size is 50%, for example – there is a simple formula for working the percentage out with a calculator: original size ÷ reproduction size × 100 = %.

ABOVE When selecting transparencies always check them with a special magnifying glass on a lightbox. This will instantly reveal any flaws or scratches on the transparency that you may otherwise not notice.

ABOVE Calculate the percentage enlargement or reduction of an image with a 'reproduction computer' or calculator.

The numbers on the outer ring of the 'reproduction computer' signify the required size and those on the inner ring the actual size. Turn the two rings until the appropriate figures meet and give the percentage.

RIGHT Always mark printing instructions for a picture clearly on an overlay. Indicate dimensions and any areas not to be printed.

SCALING AN ILLUSTRATION
1 One method is to square the image up on an overlay.

2 On the layout, define the image area to be filled and then draw a diagonal line across it.

3 Position the squared-up overlay on the layout and extend the diagonal.

4 Having established how the picture is to be cropped, mark the dimensions.

LEFT Photographers usually shoot pictures on a selection of exposures, both for safety's sake and choice.

196/A BLACK AND WHITE CUT-OUT BACKGROUND

38mm

42mm

Black and white cut-out.

Black and white cut-out on 10-percent yellow.

Black and white cut-out printed in cyan.

ABOVE Use black and white photographs creatively but always ensure that however you want them to print, your instructions are clear. Mistakes in printing are expensive to rectify.

FINAL CHECKS

■ Check your finished artwork very carefully to ensure that all your horizontals and verticals are square to each other, and that everything is correctly positioned.

■ Give your artwork a final clean.

■ Check that all your pictures are clearly marked with sizes and instructions and are enclosed with your artwork.

■ Check that all your printing instructions are clearly marked on the overlay to the artwork.

■ Put a cover-paper over the artwork – this not only gives added protection, but looks neat and professional.

■ Always get your finished artwork checked by your client before it is printed. This gives your client final responsibility to decide that the work is satisfactory.

Remember – once the job is printed there is no changing it, and if it is your fault it can cost you money and lose you a client.

TYPOGRAPHY

The graphic designer is a co-ordinator of words and images. An understanding and appreciation of typography are essential for a designer to communicate effectively. Letterforms are powerful and exciting, they can make shapes and create colour, so you must learn how to handle them with confidence. Good typography should be individual and creative.

Many of the terms we use today refer to earlier typesetting and printing techniques. You don't necessarily need to understand the mechanics of these terms to be able to use them, just as you don't need to understand how a word processor works in order to operate one. Your main consideration is to achieve aesthetic appeal and legibility. There are literally thousands of typefaces to choose from. Some are suitable to set as pages of text, while others are suitable only for decorative headlines. Each typeface has different characteristics; but they all fall into two main groups – serif faces and sans serif faces. Serif faces have little cross strokes, like tails on certain characters; sans serif faces are plain.

Typefaces are further classified into six basic groups – Gothic, Old Style, Transitional, Modern, Egyptian and Sans Serif – which roughly trace the development of type design. It is worth buying a good typeface specimen book which shows complete alphabets of many typefaces in different sizes, and examples of text setting. This will help you choose typefaces and decide on sizes.

Originally with 'moveable type', each character or letter was on a wooden or metal body of its own – and this determined the space between one character and another. With modern film photo-setting methods, this space is totally flexible. Just as with dry transfer type, letters can touch or overlap, be condensed or expanded at will. This flexibility, however, can also be a disadvantage. If typesetting is too close or too open it can be very difficult to read. This applies not only to the spaces between words and characters, but also to the spaces between lines, which is called leading.

There are three type measurements with which the designer must be familiar: points, picas and units. These measurements can be confusing in that the Anglo-American and European systems are different, although they both use the term 'point'. The art of printing spread so quickly that different type foundries cast different incompatible type, and it was not until the early 18th century that an attempt was made to standardize a system of type measurement. This happened in France, when Pierre Fournier proposed a standard unit of measurement which he called a point. These innovations were later developed by another Frenchman, called Firmin Didot, who produced a European standard. Neither Britain nor America adopted this standard, although their system was based on it.

The Anglo-American system is based on the division of one inch into 72 parts, called points and 12 points make a pica. The European (Didot) point is 0.0148 inch and 12 of these make a unit measuring 0.1776 inch. This 12-point unit is called a 'cicero' in France and Germany, a 'riga tipografica' in Italy, and an 'augustin' in Holland. There is no relationship between the Anglo-American point and the Didot point, and neither of them is based on the metric system.

An 'em' is the square of the body of a piece of type, regardless of its size. Although technically incorrect, an 'em' is often taken to mean 12 points. An 'en' is half an em. The most important measurement in controlling line length is that of each character width. This measurement is determined by dividing an em into vertical slices called set points or 'units'. Units determine not only the width of characters, but also the spaces between them. The number of units in an em varies from one typesetting system to another, but the average number is 18. The more units there are in an em, the greater the possibility of refinement.

RIGHT There are literally thousands of typefaces available to designers. The advent of advanced printing technology in the 19th century influenced type design far more than any developments in the previous 400 or so years since type had been invented.

GOTHIC
These elaborate typefaces, also known as Blackletter, originated in Germany and were derived from manuscript calligraphy. They are very difficult to read en masse.

OLD FACE
These typefaces were influenced by classical letter forms. There is little contrast between thick and thin strokes, and the wide-open characters and legibility account for their popularity today.

TRANSITIONAL
These typefaces fall between old and modern typefaces; examples such as Baskerville and Century are popular choices for book and magazine text.

MODERN FACE
The thick uprights contrast sharply with the thinner cross strokes. 'Modern' is rather misleading as these typefaces were introduced in the 18th century.

EGYPTIAN
The thickness of the serif matches that of the main letter, giving a uniform weight. Light and medium versions work very well as text setting.

SANS SERIF
This group of typefaces has no serifs and the letterforms, compared to other styles, are very uniform in character. They are a fairly recent addition to the world of type.

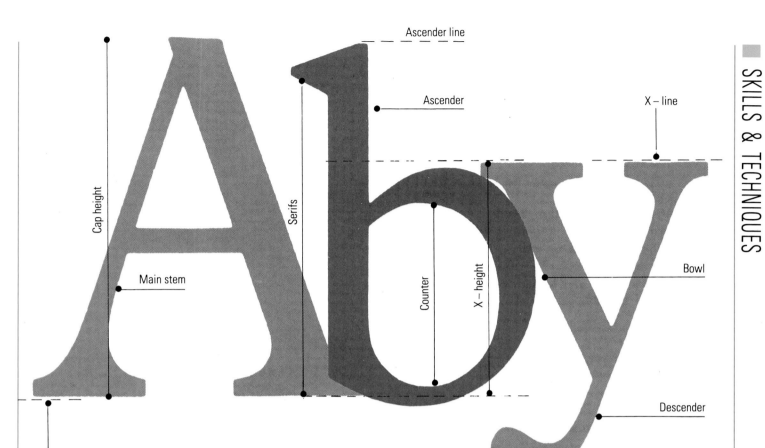

Ascender line

Ascender

X – line

Cap height

Main stem

Serifs

Counter

X – height

Bowl

Base line

Descender

Descender line

ABOVE AND RIGHT Although the terms relating to different parts of a typeset character have their origins in hot metal setting, they are still used today.

1 Width (units of set)
2 Beard (space for descender)
3 Body (point size)
4 Front
5 Foot
6 Nick
7 Height (to paper)
8 Back
9 Shoulder

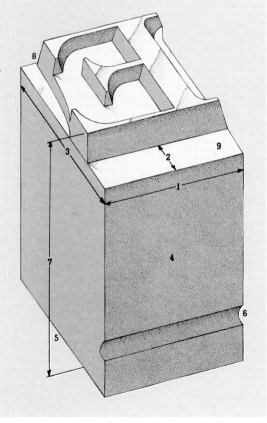

Fine rule
1 point rule
1½ point rule
3 point rule
6 point rule
3 point double medium rule
3 point shaded rule
Broken rule
Fine dotted rule
Coarse dotted rule

ABOVE Rules are straight printed lines and these are just a few of the variations.

ABOVE Until the 18th century, there was no standardization in type measurement. The 'point' as a standard unit of measurement was introduced by Pierre Fournier and developed into the standard European measurement by Firmin Didot, Britain and the United States adopted another system. In the European system a unit of 12 points is called a Cicero and in the Anglo-American system it is called a pica.

A unit system is used in phototypesetting and there are usually 18 units to 1 em, the size of the unit varying according to the size of type. The system enables very fine spacing.

Bembo justified type

Typefaces fall into two groups, those having serifs (that is, terminal projections on the stems of characters), and those without this feature, which are known as sans serif. In general, serif typefaces are easier to read for continuous text.

Helvetica range left

Typefaces fall into two groups, those having serifs (that is, terminal projections on the stems of characters), and those without this feature, which are known as sans serif. In feneral, serif typefaces are easier to read for continuous text.

Korinna range right

Typefaces fall into two groups, those having serifs (that is, terminal projections on the stems of characters), and those without this feature, which are known as sans serif. In generavl, serif typefaces are easier to read for continuous text.

Kabel centred type

Typefaces fall into two groups, those having serifs (that is, terminal projections on the stems of characters), and those without this feature, which are known as sans serif. In general, serif typefaces are easier to read for continuous text.

Bembo no leading

Typefaces fall into two groups, those having serifs (that is, terminal projections on the stems of characters), and those without this feature, which are known as sans serif. In general, serif typefaces are easier to read for continuous text.

Bembo 4 point leading

Typefaces fall into two groups, those having serifs (that is, terminal projections on the stems of characters), and those without this feature, which are known as sans serif. In general, serif typefaces are easier to read for continuous text.

LEFT Specifying type becomes much easier with experience. Always consider the function of the type so that you aim to achieve satisfying and effective results. A book set in centred type would be very difficult to read.

RIGHT Changes in the typography approach to a piece of copy can completely change the mood and feel of the words. Emphasis in typography is very important and can be achieved in numerous ways.

Typesetting is expensive, so think about what you are doing and prepare layouts before you mark up copy.

¶Producing advertisements is easy. ¶Producing advertising that sells is more difficult. ¶Producing the kind of advertising that sells and that the agency and client are proud of, takes talent, courage and teamwork. Talent from everyone in the agency. ¶There should be no-one in the agency who isn't directly concerned with improving the end product. ¶Great advertising comes only from being single-minded about what you are saying. ¶Leaving things out takes courage. ¶The agency and client are a team. Only by understanding each other's business and respecting each other's aims can they be successful. **HHCC**

PRODUCING ADVERTISEMENTS IS EASY. PRODUCING ADVERTISING THAT SELLS IS MORE DIFFICULT. ESPECIALLY WHEN MONEY IS TIGHT.

PRODUCING ADVERTISING THAT SELLS AND THAT BOTH THE AGENCY AND CLIENT ARE PROUD OF, TAKES TALENT, COURAGE AND TEAMWORK.

TALENT FROM EVERYONE IN THE AGENCY. THERE SHOULD BE NO-ONE IN THE AGENCY WHO IS NOT DIRECTLY CONCERNED WITH IMPROVING THE END PRODUCT.

GREAT ADVERTISING COMES ONLY FROM BEING SINGLE-MINDED ABOUT WHAT YOU ARE SAYING. LEAVING THINGS OUT TAKES COURAGE.

THE AGENCY AND CLIENT ARE A TEAM. ONLY BY UNDERSTANDING EACH OTHER'S BUSINESS AND RESPECTING EACH OTHER'S AIMS CAN THEY BE SUCCESSFUL.

HHCC
ADVERTISING & PUBLIC RELATIONS

COPYFITTING

This procedure enables a designer to estimate accurately how much space a manuscript will take up once it has been set. The number of words in a manuscript can only be calculated approximately, so it is advisable to round up any figures, and even to allow for a margin of error of about five or ten percent. This will take into account short lines or hyphenated words once the manuscript has been set.

It saves considerable time and money if the text is well presented. Obviously this is not always going to be the case, but it is much easier to mark up for typesetting if it is typed out clearly, and much easier for the typesetter to read. If you decide not to cast off your copy you may have to have the whole job reset so that it fits the design. This is expensive and time consuming, so it pays to get it right first time.

Begin by estimating the number of characters in your typed manuscript – a character is a letter, a punctuation mark or a space between words. If you hold an imperial ruler under a line of typing, you will find that to every inch you will usually get 10 or 12 characters (depending on the typewriter). Count the number of characters in, say, 10 lines, divide that number by 10 and you have an average character count per line. Multiply this by the number of lines on the page to give you an estimate of the number of characters on that page.

If you are dealing with a large manuscript you can apply the same process to working out an average character count per page. If you count the number of characters on, say the first 10 pages (assuming they are fairly representative pages) and divide that total by 10, you arrive at an average. By multiplying that average by the number of pages in your manuscript you have a fairly good estimate of your total number of characters. This figure is also useful when estimating the cost of your typesetting.

The next step is to establish how much space the manuscript will fill when typeset. This will vary according to the typeface and the type size you have chosen. By measuring the length of the lower case alphabet, in a specimen book, in the appropriate face and size, you will discover that 26

CASTING OFF COPY

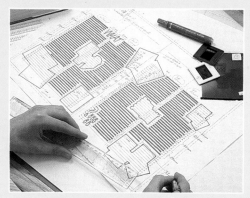

1 Estimating the number of characters and lines that a piece of copy will occupy in its typeset form is called 'casting off'. Always establish the layout before you mark up copy.

2 Once you have calculated the number of characters in a piece of text, you are in a position to work out which typeface and type size is required. Many type manufacturers supply sets of tables to help you.

characters take up, let us say, 30mm. If you measure the length of the line you wish to typeset to, in millimetres, divide by 30 and multiply by 26, that will give you the number of characters in that line. Measure the number of lines in your design with a depth scale (type rule), and you can calculate the number of typeset characters. This figure can be changed by altering your type size, typeface or length of line.

Many type manufacturers supply special sets of tables to make this process easier. Different typesetting systems produce different numbers of characters in a line. When copyfitting refer to actual alphabets produced by the system you will be using.

Typesetting instructions must be clearly written on a manuscript, in a way that a typesetter can understand. These instructions, or mark-up, should specify the following: the typeface, its size and leading, the length of line, or 'measure', and any typographic variations such as capitals, italic, bold, small capitals, underlining, rules, etc. If the manuscript is complicated, it is a good idea to write a master style sheet for reference, with all this information on it.

There is a standard system of marks which you should use when marking up copy. It is a common language between designers and typesetters and you must familiarize yourself with it. If you are unsure about the effectiveness of an instruction, talk to the typesetter about it and supply a typographic layout for him to follow, if you think it is necessary.

The first piece of typesetting you will get back is called a 'galley proof'. This is your last opportunity to check details such as spelling and to change the styling, so be as thorough as possible. Supply your client with a copy of this, too, for him to read. When you are satisfied with the alterations you have made, add them to your client's copy of the galley and return this to the typesetter for him to run out the final galley.

In theory this should be pasted down on the artwork as a clean galley, but it is very common for last-minute changes to occur, so sometimes it will be necessary to run out the galley a third time. Once the artwork is complete, small changes can still be made with line strips, that is, cutting out the incorrect line by hand and pasting a corrected one in its place.

TIP

When curving typesetting, apply adhesive to the back so that the strip of setting will stay secure, then cut between each letter leaving it joined to the others only at the bottom edge. Cut right through if you need to as you place each letter in position.

LEFT A tracing overlay is useful for protecting your work and as an instruction sheet. Before you send any job out, always check your instructions carefully.

RIGHT Proof correction marks are a standard method of communication. Proofs that are being corrected should be marked in the margin as well as in the text. This is because the typesetter always looks down the margin to see where the corrections occur.

One of the most difficult stages in your career will be replacing your college work with commercially printed specimens. When you begin looking for work, very little, if anything, of what you have done will be printed and suitable for proving to potential clients that you are capable of turning your ideas into print. It is the appearance of your work in print which is the measure of your ability and success. The end result of nearly all commissions is a printed image. Beautiful, slick presentation and visuals will impress your client, but are, ultimately, useless if you are not able to transfer them into print successfully.

The ability to look at a piece of artwork and visualize the finished printed product, comes only with experience. At the beginning of your career, you will find it difficult to judge how two colours will look together, or how small a type size you can reverse white out of solid black before it fills in. Printing technology is very complex, and different processes produce quite different results, so it is essential to choose the correct printing method for your job. A job which has been silk-screened and looks terrific may appear totally different when printed by lithography, for example. It is possible to print on almost any surface, but it is important to understand the techniques, what the results will be like, and which method of reproduction is most appropriate.

The other consideration, before you commit yourself to a printer and a particular process, will be cost. Sometimes you may have to rethink your ideas in order to make them more economical to produce, so when you are visualizing a job be aware of costs. Before talking to your client, consult your printer about what you want to achieve – especially if you are using a particular process for the first time. There are four principle methods:

■ In relief printing, paper is pressed onto a raised area of wood or metal, which has been inked. Commercially this is known as letterpress. It is the oldest method of printing, dating back to the Middle Ages, and is, basically, the same way that Johann Gutenberg produced printed copies of the Bible *c* 1455.

PROOF CORRECTION MARKS

INSTRUCTION TO PRINTER	TEXTUAL MARK	MARGINAL MARK
Correction is concluded	none	
Leave unchanged	typeface groups	
Remove unwanted marks	typeface groups	
Push down risen spacing material	typeface groups	
Refer to appropriate authority	typeface groups	
Insert new material	typeface groups	new matter followed by
Insert additional material	typegroups	
Delete	typeface groups	
Delete and close up	typeface groups	
Substitute character or part of one or more words	topeface groups	
Wrong fount: replace with correct fount	typeface groups	
Correct damaged characters	typeface groups	
Transpose words	groups typeface	
Transpose characters	ypteface groups	
Transpose lines	the dimension of is disastrous when	
Transpose lines (2)	the dimension of is disastrous when	
Centre type	typeface groups	
Indent 1 em	typeface groups	(1em)
Range left	typeface groups	
Set line or column justified	typeface groups	
Move matter to right	typeface groups	
Move matter to left	typeface groups	
Take down to next line	typeface groups	
Take back to previous line	typeface groups	
Raise matter	typeface groups	
Lower matter	typeface groups	
Correct vertical alignment	typeface groups	
Correct horizontal alignment	typeface groups	
Close up space	typeface groups	
Insert space between words	typefacegroups	
Reduce space between words	typeface groups	
Reduce or insert space between letters	type facegroups	
Make space appear equal	typeface groups	

INSTRUCTION TO PRINTER	TEXTUAL MARK	MARGINAL MARK
Insert space between lines	aerobic movement. The dimensions of	+#
Reduce space between paragraphs	aerobic movement. The dimensions of	−#
Insert parentheses or brackets	typeface groups	
Figure or abbreviation to be spelled out in full	12 point twelve pt	sp. out
Move matter to position indicated	are called the set points dimension	
Set in or change to italics	typeface groups	
Set in or change to capitals	typeface groups	
Set in or change to small capitals	typeface groups	
Capitals for initials, small caps for rest of word	typeface groups	
Set in or change to bold type	typeface groups	
Set in or change to bold italic type	typeface groups	
Change capitals to lower case	typefACE groups	
Change small capitals to lower case	typeface GROUPS	
Change italics to roman	typeface groups	
Invert type	typeface groups	
Insert ligature	filmsetter	fi
Substitute separate letters for ligature	filmsetter	fi
Insert period	typeface groups	(.)
Insert colon	typeface groups	(:)
Insert semicolon	typeface groups	;
Insert comma	typeface groups	,
Insert quotation marks	typeface groups	
Insert double quotation marks	typeface groups	
Insert character in superior position	typeface groups	
Substitute character in inferior position	typeface groups	
Insert apostrophe	typeface groups	
Insert ellipsis	typeface groups	...000
Insert leader dots	typeface groups	⊙⊙⊙ =
Insert hyphen	typefacegroups	= - =
Insert rule	typeface groups	(2pt -)
Insert oblique	typeface groups	/
Start new paragraph	are called points. The questions	
Run on	are called points. The question is	

63

Relief printing

Intaglio printing

Lithographic printing

Stencil printing

■ Lithographic printing is the youngest printing process and works on the principle that oil and water do not mix. The areas of the litho plates which are to print are made oily, so the ink sticks to them, and the non-image areas are kept damp, so the ink is repelled.

■ Gravure, or intaglio, printing is the reverse of letterpress. The areas of the image to print are recessed, or etched, into the metal plate. The entire surface of the plate is covered with ink then wiped clean, leaving the recess filled with ink. The image is then transferred onto paper by a combination of absorption and adhesion. This process has been used by artists and engravers for over 200 years.

■ Stencil printing is one of the oldest ways of duplication and works by pressing ink onto paper through a cut-out shape. These shapes are held in place by a fine mesh or screen, so the process is known as screen printing.

LETTERPRESS

A letterpress printing surface may consist of type alone, or type and photo-engraved plates. These plates are used if an illustration or picture is to be printed, and can be made of zinc, copper, magnesium or plastic. The picture is etched onto one of these plates, which is then mounted onto another surface called a block to make it the same thickness as the type.

The type and blocks are then assembled and locked together in a framework called a forme. Corrections can be carried out right up to the time the press is about to run, a great advantage of letterpress printing.

From a design point of view, you have less control over the job because areas of text are positioned by the printer. Each letter is on its own little block of metal, so it is difficult and expensive to do very exciting things typographically, such as overlap letters. It is a process used chiefly for daily newspapers or quite small printing jobs such as simple business cards. Letterpress is gradually being replaced by lithography because better quality can be achieved.

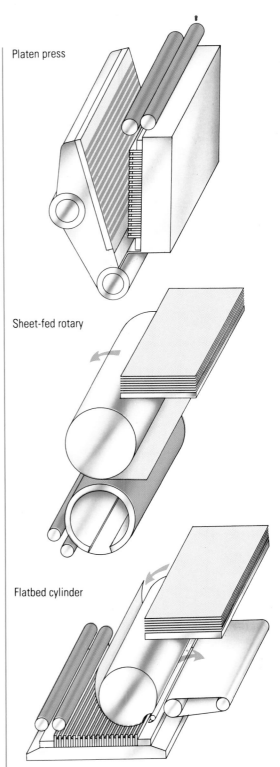

Platen press

Sheet-fed rotary

Flatbed cylinder

LEFT Study and understand the four basic methods of printing an image so that you can choose the most suitable. Take into account the number of copies you require and the quality.

ABOVE The simplest letterpress machine is the platen press. When the press opens the vertical forme is inked by rollers, and when it closes again the paper is pressed against the inked surface. The sheet fed-rotary will print sheets of various sizes at a speed which can be regulated. In the flatbed cylinder press, inked rollers ink the flat forme and a rotating pressure cylinder presses the paper against the type.

ABOVE Copper plates are most suitable for fine halftone work. The dots are arranged in lines and are larger where the shadows are darker.

RIGHT Plates made of zinc are much cheaper. Both of these plates are mounted onto wood.

LITHOGRAPHY

This is now the most common and widely used printing process, employing machinery ranging from small office duplicating machines, to massive presses which are used to print magazines, books and newspapers. The process was first invented by a German typographer called Alos Senefelder at the beginning of the 19th century. Originally the printing surface was polished stone and images were drawn directly onto it with a greasy crayon.

In litho printing nowadays, printing surfaces referred to as plates are used, made from zinc, aluminium, plastic, paper, copper and chromium. The most popular is aluminium which is strong, light and economic to use. In the commercial process, the ink is transferred from the plate onto a rubber blanket, which is then pressed against the paper. This is called offset lithography because the image is not transferred directly to the paper from the plate.

Lithography offers a wide choice of print quality to the designer and most work that a designer handles will be printed this way. The designer provides camera-ready artwork, from which the printer makes film and then plates. Unlike letterpress, the designer has total control over the work because the printer follows the layout or artwork instructions exactly.

1 The image to be printed is treated with a greasy medium and raised. The plate is then dampened with rollers.
2 The plate is rolled with ink which adheres to the greasy image.
3 Paper is laid onto the inked plate.
4 Both paper and plate are run through the press.
5 The pressure transfers the ink to the paper and gives the finished print.

ABOVE In photolithography the design to be printed is transferred photographically to a plate.

BELOW In offset lithography the ink is offset from the plate to a rubber blanket before it is transferred to the paper. The soft rubber surface gives a cleaner printed image than the plate.

65

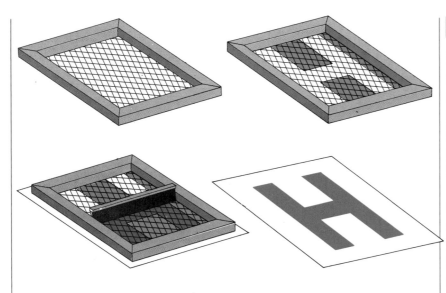

SCREEN PRINTING

This process is one of the simplest printing methods, and is economical if the print run is quite small. A stencil is held in position on a screen of stretched fabric and ink is forced through the stencil and mesh of the screen by means of a squeegee. Traditionally the screen was made from silk, whence the term silk-screen printing derives, but it has been largely replaced with synthetic materials. Stencils for commercial screen printing are made photographically by the printer from artwork supplied by the designer. It is an especially good method of printing from hand-drawn artwork, and a very simple operation to set up in a small workshop of your own.

From the designer's point of view, screen printing offers an interesting technique for certain work. The ink is applied very thickly and has a dense quality, so it is very suitable for printing light colours onto dark surfaces. Although technology facilitates high-speed screen printing, it still tends to be a hand-operated process used on short runs. The texture of the screen is quite restrictive and the process is not suitable for reproducing fine halftones. The main advantages of screen printing is that it is versatile and can print on almost any surface, such as wood, glass, metal, plastic and fabrics. For these reasons it is a popular method of producing exhibition stands, point-of-sale displays, posters and PVC stickers.

ABOVE In silkscreen printing a stencil is held in position on a screen.
1 A fine gauze screen is stretched over a wooden frame.
2 The stencil of the design is placed over the screen.
3 Paper is put under the screen and ink drawn across it with a squeegee.
4 The ink passes through the stencil to make the image.

GRAVURE PRINTING

Gravure is mostly used for printing high-quality magazines or fine art illustration, where the quality of reproduction is of paramount importance. It is also used for printing packaging, cellophane (acetate), decorative laminates, wallpaper and postage stamps. The finished results are superb, but the costs are prohibitive.

The image to be printed is etched in a pattern of small cells onto a cylindrical copper plate. These cells can be of varying size and depth and they act as wells to hold the ink. Cells can vary in depth from 1/200,000–$\frac{1}{6}$ inch (0.0001–0.4mm), so a considerable range of tone and colour graduation is possible. The volume of the cells determines how much ink passes onto the paper – the deeper the cell, the denser the inking.

For the designer, gravure gives excellent results, but its use is rarely necessary, because lithography now usually offers adequate printing quality, and clients are not often prepared to pay the extra costs. The greatest disadvantage of gravure is the considerable cost of corrections once the plate has been made. Gravure is commonly used for magazine and high-quality, long-run brochure and catalogue work.

OTHER PRINT PROCESSES

Flexography is a relief printing process, like letterpress, but the printing surfaces are made of rubber. The method is ideal for printing packaging, especially packaging for food, for which special inks have been developed. It is always advisable to talk to the printer before preparing artwork, because a certain amount of distortion takes place between the artwork stage and the final rubber plates. It is not suitable for reproducing fine detail

Thermography produces a glossy, raised image. It is used mostly on business stationery and the result can resemble embossing if it is done well. Cheap thermography always looks bad because the type spreads and appears very uneven. Inks in a new range of colours have been developed and these may help to increase the popularity of thermography.

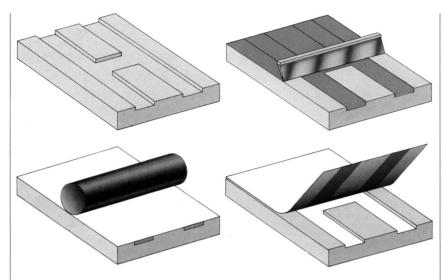

Die stamping creates a raised printed image, but the results are always much sharper than thermography. The design is hand-cut or photo-enlarged from artwork onto a metal plate called a die. Die stamping is used extensively in the production of high-quality stationery.

Embossing produces a raised image by using a recessed die without inks. The image is normally printed in colour first, using one of the main printing processes, then embossed. An image which stands out in relief but is not inked is described as 'blind embossed'.

Foil blocking is also known as hot-foil printing and hot-foil stamping. Bright durable foils are pressed onto paper with a heated die. The foils come in a wide range of colours, have a highly reflective quality, and when used sparingly can look very lavish. The process is most often seen on mass-market paperback covers.

WHICH METHOD TO USE

I have briefly discussed the various methods and techniques used to create a printed image. It is very important to understand each of them, what they are suitable for, and the results they achieve. When you receive a commission to design a leaflet or brochure, for example, your choice of process will depend on your budget – you will not always be able to afford full colour printing, nor will it always be the most suitable solution.

ABOVE In intaglio printing the ink is pressed into a recessed design.
1 The design is engraved into the plate.
2 The plate is inked with rollers and surplus ink removed by drawing a thin blade across the plate.
3 paper is then laid onto the plate and pressure applied by a rubber coated roller.
4 The paper is forced into the recesses so that the ink is transfered onto the paper making the print.

Single colour printing usually means printing black ink onto white paper. However, always try to make the best use of one colour. Consider using tints as well, a range of greys for example, from light grey to solid black. Tints are described as percentages of the solid colour(s) and are printed as areas of dots. The dots are very small, and the more dots there are within a set area, the darker the tint, so 50% black is darker than 10% black.

Of course, the one colour you use for a single-colour job does not have to be black, nor does the paper have to be white. By using another colour of ink or paper, you can achieve a completely different result. When you specify a particular colour to a printer use the Pantone colour selector. This is an internationally recognized colour matching system. Using the selector, a designer can specify a colour to a printer working anywhere in the world, simply by quoting a reference number. The selector, will show a wide range of colours printed on both matt and glossy papers. The more expensive selectors have little squares of the colour which you can tear off and attach to your artwork. There are other Pantone products too, such as printed papers, films and markers, which can be used when visualizing a job. This makes it easier to transfer the colours in a visual into print.

Two-colour printing can appear very colourful given the imaginative use of two colours. Always be positive about printing restrictions and use them to your advantage. The clever use of tints and overprinting can make two colours seem much more colourful.

RIGHT Tints of colour consist of tiny dots of varying density. The higher the density of dots, the darker the tint. By using tints and overprinting tints you can achieve a vast range of effects and colours.

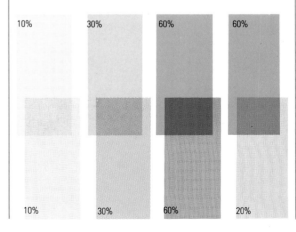

ABOVE A halftone is an image produced using a 'screen' – a glass sheet engraved with lines or dots in a regular pattern. A continuous tone original photographed through this sort of screen produces an image consisting of dots.

ABOVE If you magnify a halftone the dot pattern will become clearly visible.

LEFT By printing a halftone in different colours or over a tint of another colour, you can vary the effect quite dramatically. Another way of achieving a colour effect with a black and white halftone is to print a 'duotone'. A duotone is a two-colour halftone made from a black and white original. The original is photographed twice to produce a black halftone and the middle tones in a second colour. The two can be combined in varying proportions.

Black halftone

Black halftone over 10% yellow

Black halftone printed cyan

Black halftone magenta

40% colour duotone

Full colour value duotone

To reproduce colour pictures you will have to use four-colour printing. Yellow, cyan, magenta and black are known as the 'process colours' or the four-colour set. By mixing these colours together in varying proportions, determined by the size of the half-tone dots, you can obtain virtually all shades of any colour. For very specialist reproduction work, such as fine art paintings, or if you want metallic gold or silver, a fifth supplementary colour may be added, but for most jobs, the four process colours are adequate.

Four printing plates are made which print the proportional amount of each colour in each area of the image. Together they build up the combination of colour in the final reproduction. To make these plates it is necessary to separate the original into four photographic images which represent the relative values of each colour. This stage is called origination or colour separation and is usually carried out by a reproduction, or origination, house. The four images are now recorded on film, the size of the final reproduction, which are then screened. The screening process breaks the image into a series of dots of varying sizes, which record all the shades of colour in the original – it is not possible to print varying tones of colour using different in- tensities of ink in lithography. Colour separation can be done directly or indirectly using a camera, or by using an electronic scanner. Both methods are widely used, but scanning is rapidly replacing camera origination.

The four separate sheets of film produced by the scanning process should register with each other, that is, the images should be absolutely identical in size when the films are superimposed on each other, and the same size as the image you want to print. The films are checked for colour accuracy and made into four separate plates, one for each colour, from which the four colours are printed.

Imperfections in printing inks make it impossible to produce perfect colour reproduction without some correcting, so when a job is being prepared colour proofs are produced. These enable you to check the accurate reproduction of the original before it is printed. Once you have looked at the

Yellow printer	Magenta printer	Cyan printer	Black printer
Yellow proof	Magenta proof	Cyan proof	Black proof
Yellow proof	Yellow plus magenta	Yellow, magenta plus cyan	Yellow, magenta, cyan black

ABOVE In four-colour printing the image is photographed four times, once through each colour filter, to produce the separation negatives. When the four negatives are proofed in the individual colours and combined they result in a full-colour image.

LEFT If you magnify a full-colour printed image you will clearly see the pattern of overlapping dots that together make up the reproduction.

BOTTOM LEFT It is essential in two-, three- and four-colour printing that the dots are arranged at the correct angles.

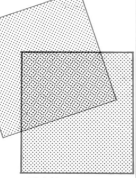

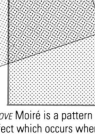

ABOVE Moiré is a pattern effect which occurs when dotted screens are placed at the wrong angles. The pattern distorts the image, and makes it difficult to read.

proofs under good daylight or under lights which have no colour bias, write your comments on the proofs as clearly as you can. For example, if the proof looks too red, suggest that the film is corrected, or that the amount of red ink is reduced during the printing. There are other more technical methods by which you can instruct the colour repro house to reduce or increase a precise amount of a particular colour which you can learn later. If major colour correction is necessary, the original may have to be rescanned or re-separated. If you are particularly dissatisfied ask for another proof. If your proofing has not been done by a printer you may expect a slight variation in ink density when the job is printed. This is particularly true of web-offset printing, where the ink builds up. The safest way to check is to ask for 'machine proofs'; the printer will provide proofs using the equipment the job will be printed on. They are usually more expensive, but they are a more accurate reproduction of the final printed job.

ABOVE When you are working in four-colour the printer will provide you with colour proofs. They must be checked carefully to ensure there are no blemishes or spots, that they are the right size, fit, in register and that the colour is right.

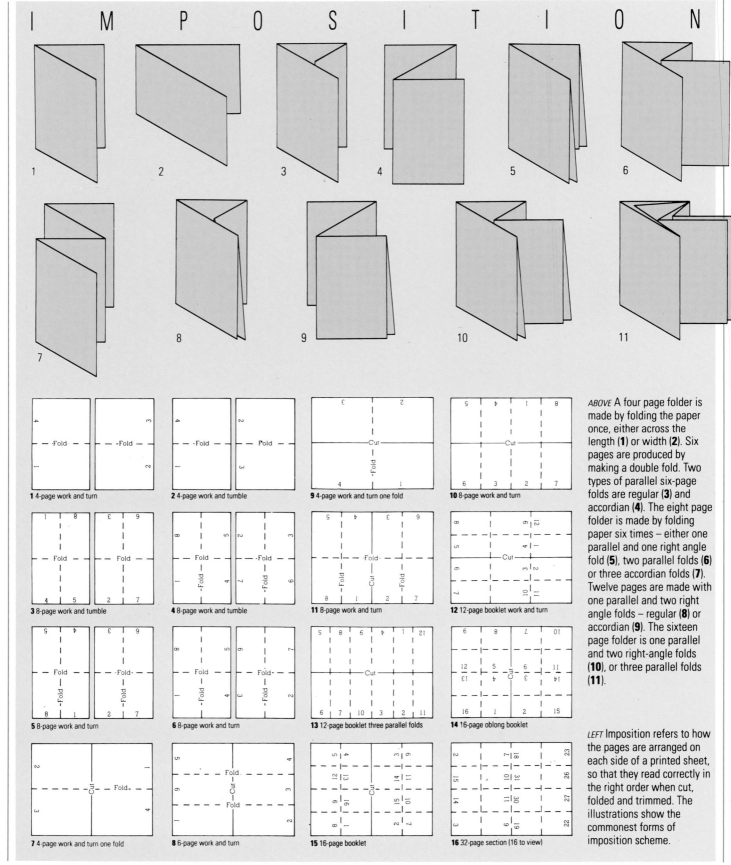

1 4-page work and turn

2 4-page work and tumble

9 4-page work and turn one fold

10 8-page work and turn

3 8-page work and tumble

4 8-page work and tumble

11 8-page work and turn

12 12-page booklet work and turn

5 8-page work and turn

6 8-page work and turn

13 12-page booklet three parallel folds

14 16-page oblong booklet

7 4-page work and turn one fold

8 6-page work and turn

15 16-page booklet

16 32-page section (16 to view)

ABOVE A four page folder is made by folding the paper once, either across the length (**1**) or width (**2**). Six pages are produced by making a double fold. Two types of parallel six-page folds are regular (**3**) and accordian (**4**). The eight page folder is made by folding paper six times – either one parallel and one right angle fold (**5**), two parallel folds (**6**) or three accordian folds (**7**). Twelve pages are made with one parallel and two right angle folds – regular (**8**) or accordian (**9**). The sixteen page folder is one parallel and two right-angle folds (**10**), or three parallel folds (**11**).

LEFT Imposition refers to how the pages are arranged on each side of a printed sheet, so that they read correctly in the right order when cut, folded and trimmed. The illustrations show the commonest forms of imposition scheme.

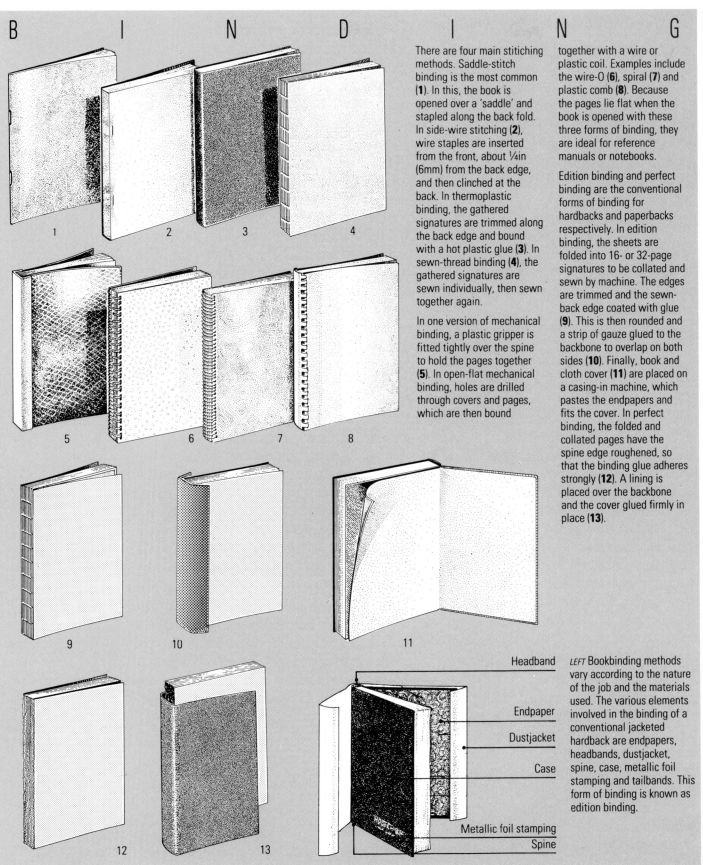

B I N D I N G

There are four main stitiching methods. Saddle-stitch binding is the most common (**1**). In this, the book is opened over a 'saddle' and stapled along the back fold. In side-wire stitching (**2**), wire staples are inserted from the front, about ¼in (6mm) from the back edge, and then clinched at the back. In thermoplastic binding, the gathered signatures are trimmed along the back edge and bound with a hot plastic glue (**3**). In sewn-thread binding (**4**), the gathered signatures are sewn individually, then sewn together again.

In one version of mechanical binding, a plastic gripper is fitted tightly over the spine to hold the pages together (**5**). In open-flat mechanical binding, holes are drilled through covers and pages, which are then bound together with a wire or plastic coil. Examples include the wire-O (**6**), spiral (**7**) and plastic comb (**8**). Because the pages lie flat when the book is opened with these three forms of binding, they are ideal for reference manuals or notebooks.

Edition binding and perfect binding are the conventional forms of binding for hardbacks and paperbacks respectively. In edition binding, the sheets are folded into 16- or 32-page signatures to be collated and sewn by machine. The edges are trimmed and the sewn-back edge coated with glue (**9**). This is then rounded and a strip of gauze glued to the backbone to overlap on both sides (**10**). Finally, book and cloth cover (**11**) are placed on a casing-in machine, which pastes the endpapers and fits the cover. In perfect binding, the folded and collated pages have the spine edge roughened, so that the binding glue adheres strongly (**12**). A lining is placed over the backbone and the cover glued firmly in place (**13**).

Headband
Endpaper
Dustjacket
Case
Metallic foil stamping
Spine

LEFT Bookbinding methods vary according to the nature of the job and the materials used. The various elements involved in the binding of a conventional jacketed hardback are endpapers, headbands, dustjacket, spine, case, metallic foil stamping and tailbands. This form of binding is known as edition binding.

BUYING PRINT

Printing is usually the most expensive single item involved in a job, so it is essential that you take care to ensure that you get the results you want. The way in which your artwork is printed will determine the success or failure of the job, so remember this when deciding on a printer. Don't always go for the cheapest price!

Once you have completed the design and know what is involved, you can ask several suitable printers for quotations. If you are using a printer for the first time, ask to see samples of work he has done. The best way to get an accurate price is to show the printer a visual of the job, or your artwork. Explain the job carefully to him, and don't leave any information out – you could find yourself with extra expenses if you do. Confirm the number of illustrations, the format, type of binding, paper, how many colour proofs you want, and the quantity.

At the same time make sure that you both agree how your work is to be presented – there are different ways of doing certain things and a printer will have preferences. The less work involved for the printer, the cheaper the job. For example, when you are printing tints, you can lay these yourself or you can get the printer to do them. Whichever you do, make sure that you both know it, so when the final print bill comes in you are not paying more than you budgeted for. In fact, if you discuss the job properly and well in advance, the printer may be able to suggest simple changes which could save you money. Always remember to ask for the quotation in writing and when you decide which printer to use, write an order with your terms and delivery dates clearly stated.

Deciding on which paper, or stock, to use for a job is a matter of budget, experience and knowledge of paper ranges. A printer is always happy to show you samples, and even other jobs printed on the same stock, but it is wise to put yourself onto paper manufacturers' mailing lists. Printers will usually use one paper wholesaler for most deliveries, and not all papers are readily available, or kept by all wholesalers. Part of your responsibility as a designer is to look after details like paper – a good quality paper or one with an interesting surface can make the final result far more distinguished. If you are undecided, ask the printer to provide you with proofs of the job on several different samples of paper. This way you are able to make direct comparisons.

If you are on a very limited budget or have a tight deadline on a job, you can save both time and money, by visiting the printer yourself and adjusting the colour as the job is being printed. The first time you work with a particular printer, it is a good idea to go and see your job on the press anyway.

When the job is complete, clarify the delivery address and how you want the job packed. Never allow a job to be delivered to a client before you have looked at the finished result. If anything is wrong, you have an opportunity to stop delivery and do something about it. Never take delivery of a job before you are completely satisfied. Bad finishing can make a job totally unacceptable. You will be judged on the final printed result, so do not leave anything to chance. A job that goes wrong during printing can lose you a client and cost you money.

If you are working on your own, you may not be able to afford to pay the printer before you have been paid by your client. If you have not worked with your customer before, it is a good idea to ask them to pay the printer direct. Not all clients are prompt payers and you may find yourself with a large print bill and a reluctant client. If you order print you are legally liable to pay for it. It is perfectly acceptable business practice to ask your client to pay the print bill and for you to charge a handling fee. This should be discussed in the early stages of negotiation. It is also acceptable for you to ask for an advance on a job to cover your expenses if you haven't worked with someone before.

RIGHT Buying print is difficult to do well and is a service which should be charged for. Either add a commission onto the print price when you invoice the job, or if the client is paying direct, agree a handling fee. A job which is late or badly produced threatens your livelihood and reputation.

This checklist is designed to avoid a few of the problems you may encounter when dealing with printers.

PRINTING CHECKLIST

- ■ **Agree schedule and price with printer**

- ■ **Who is responsible for payment?**

- ■ **Clarify how your artwork should be presented**

- ■ **Have you specified paper?**

- ■ **Check that the proofs are correct for content**

- ■ **Have all your instructions been followed?**

- ■ **Are tints laid correctly and accurately?**

- ■ **Is the line reproduction sharp?**

- ■ **Are pictures the correct size?**

- ■ **Have you checked proofs for alignment?**

- ■ **Check trim marks and folds**

- ■ **Are the proofs correct colour values?**

- ■ **Are your colour corrections clearly marked?**

- ■ **Will a second proof be required?**

- ■ **If there are alterations, who will pay for them?**

- ■ **Show your client a proof and get their approval**

- ■ **Check the final job before it is delivered**

- ■ **Have you clarified delivery details?**

- ■ **Phone the client and get confirmation that they are satisfied.**

T I P

GRIDS

Grids are devised and used to enable designers to be consistent in their layout. If you are designing a magazine, book or large catalogue, there are certain elements which will be the same on every page, such as the position of page numbers or the width of margins.

Once you have styled a typical page of a book or magazine, you will have decided on page size, margins, position and size of text, column widths and number of columns. You may decide that on some pages you want two columns, but on others five.

Assess all the possible standard requirements and draw up a piece of line artwork with all this information on it. It is better to supply too much information than not enough. When drawing in the lines representing your text, you may want to number them so that if you are discussing text over the phone with an editor or author who has a copy of your layout, you can refer to specific lines on the page. A grid is also essential for illustrators, photographers, typesetters and printers who are working on the book.

If the job is a fairly small one, pencil grids will be sufficient, and you can draw these up by hand. However, 'the design of anything with a large number of pages necessitates using printed grids. Make sure the grid is accurate and point out to the printer that they must check reproduction size very carefully when making plates. It need only be very slightly inaccurate to be highly frustrating to use or, worse, useless.

When you have a grid printed, it is a good idea to have two sets prepared – one on transparent layout or tracing paper, and the other on artboard. The transparent one can be used for laying the book out and tracing in the illustrations, and the artboard version can be used for pasting up the camera-ready copy. You can use a transparent grid on an enlarger with ease when scaling illustrations. This then becomes an overlay and position guide for the pictures when presenting the camera-ready boards to the printer. When pasting-up the artwork onto the artboards, use the light box to position text rather than the parallel motion. The sheer

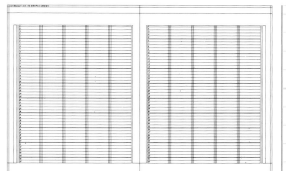

LEFT Pre-printed grid sheets make the task of positioning copy and pictures much quicker. The lines are printed in pale blue and are not picked up when a negative of the artwork is made.
I have actually printed the grid lines over this spread to give an idea of how useful a grid can be.

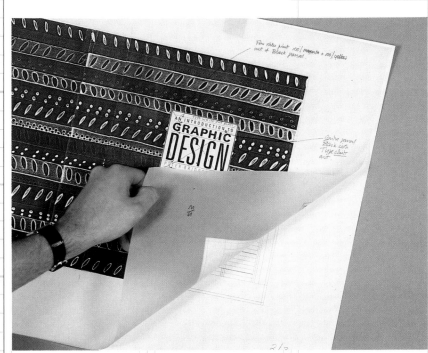

ABOVE Use your trace grid for layout work and printing instructions and your art board grid for all your black and white line artwork.

number of pages will demand this. By placing the grid on the light box you will be able to see the lines through the repro proofs. This enables you to position text quickly and accurately.

Have the grid sheets printed in pale blue (photographic blue) as the grid lines will not be picked up when a negative is made from the finished artwork.

If you are ever asked to prepare very precise miniature 'flow-charts', you can reduce the grid to the required size. This way you effectively design a book in miniature very accurately and can judge exactly how many lines of text are required.

You must always remember that a grid is only there to make your life easier. It should never be regarded as a design straitjacket and should be disregarded if an idea demands it.

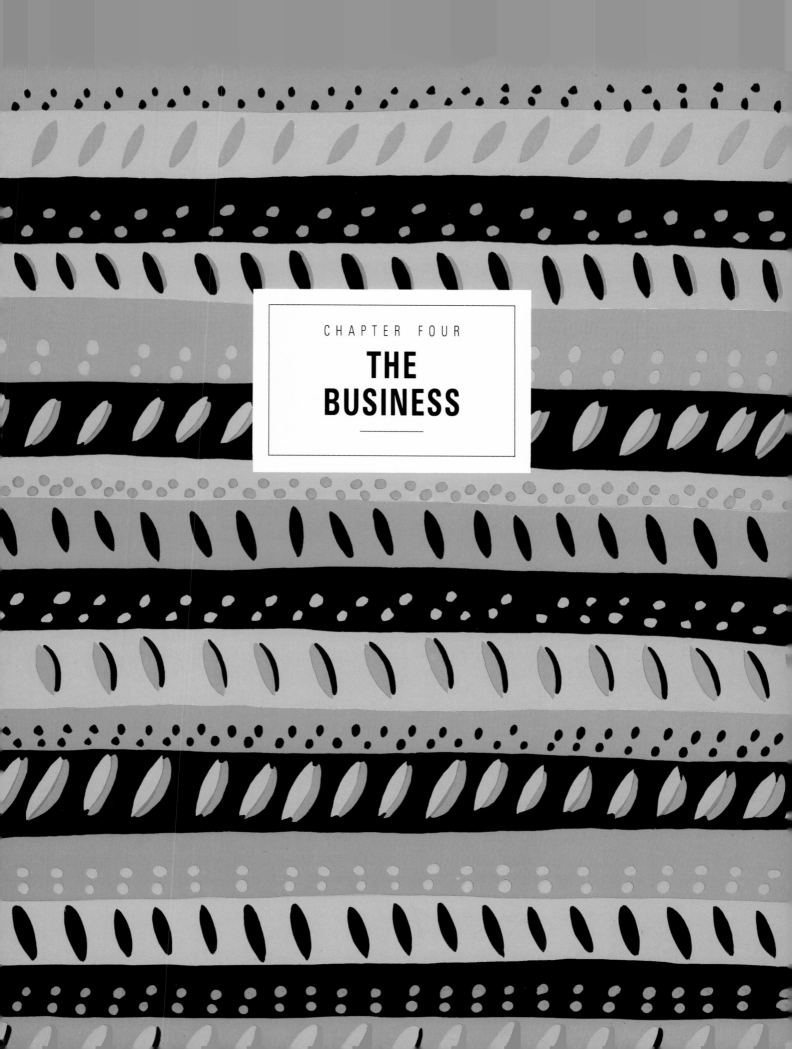

CHAPTER FOUR

THE BUSINESS

The career opportunities for a graphic designer are quite diverse, but you will find that similar kinds of visual and aesthetic judgements apply to most sectors of the commercial design industry. Your main objective is always to communicate information to your audience effectively. The differences between, let us say, working in television and working in publishing, are the technology and the technical expertise required. These can only be learned by working in and understanding that industry.

YOUR PORTFOLIO

Your work and its presentation is essential to your success. This cannot be stressed enough. When you walk into an office for the first time, your portfolio is an instant communication, not only of your skill and talent as a designer, but also that you are a professional and you mean business.

The commercial world is a busy place, people are always in a hurry. Your work must be clearly presented if people are going to bother looking at it. An effective way of doing this is to display your samples flat, in a ring binder with transparent sleeves. This method not only protects your work, but also makes it easy to look through. You can mount your samples onto sheets of coloured paper (if in doubt, use black) and slip these into transparent sleeves.

Colour transparencies should be mounted in black window boards or plastic sleeves, so that they can be examined in groups. If you want a brochure to be handled, keep one mounted flat in its sleeve, and carry another with you at the back of the folder.

Keep your portfolio up to date with recent work, not what you have done over the last five years. But if you have little recent work available, put together some self-motivated ideas. It will demonstrate creativity and enthusiasm.

It's important that you don't try and show every single piece of work you've ever done. Be selective – people won't have time to see your total professional life flash before them – and think about who you are showing your work to, and, therefore, what would be relevant. You may have to change the contents of your portfolio for every interview.

AT AN INTERVIEW

When you have arranged an interview, with an art director for example, never be late. Remember how important your personal presentation is. Many businesses are quite conservative and people do make judgements about personality based on appearance. This is a foolish thing to do, but for the sake of getting work present yourself in the best possible way and don't be late for the appointment. During the interview allow people time to look through your work at their own pace. Explain the contents of your folder as they go through it, but try not to talk incessantly – some art directors are happy to look quietly through a portfolio without a running commentary.

If you are unable to arrange an interview with a prospective client or employer you can always give them samples of your previous work. If your work is suitable for photocopying, make up a little package of photocopied specimens and leave them together with a business card and a *curriculum vitae* (resumé).

> **You may also find the life insular unless you are working in a studio with other people – which will also help you share the costs of equipment. As your income will not be regular you may find it difficult to afford or arrange holidays, especially while you are building up the business.**

LEFT When you prepare your portfolio ensure that the work displayed in it is relevant to the person you are seeing. Your portfolio is the first communication of your skill as a designer and should demonstrate that you are a professional.

FREELANCING

Many designers work as 'freelancers'. This means working for different clients on a job-by-job basis, usually from home or a separate rented studio. Most freelancers begin by working from home, because it is the most cost-effective and convenient way. You save on overheads and you can claim a proportion of your household expenses against tax. You should consider employing an accountant if you need advice about tax as a self-employed person.

Before you begin working from home, think carefully about practical considerations. It is all very well setting up a studio in the living room, but is working late into the night in order to meet a deadline going to upset others at home? Unless you have a separate telephone number for your business, and this is unlikely, clients will be able to call you any time, and they do. Will you mind?

Plan a studio in the home carefully. The space must be suitable for the job. Obviously, setting aside a separate room is the best way, but not always practical. Considerations such as clients visiting the home must be taken into account – if you are working in the top room of a house, clients will have to walk through the rest of your home to get there – do you mind this?

If you decide on renting a separate studio, the first consideration is whether you can afford it? One of the cheapest ways of separating your work life from your home life is to rent studio space or desk space in an existing studio. For a fairly small amount of money you can rent not only the area, but also facilities that you may not have, such as a PMT camera (stat camera) and darkroom, a photocopier or a fax. It may also be convenient for the studio to supply you with work, and this can be useful while you are building up your own contacts. However, take care to clarify any arrangement and commitments like this before you move in.

This arrangement has other advantages, too. Working with other people can be of a great benefit creatively; it provides an opportunity for discussing and exchanging ideas. Some clients will also be more impressed if you have a separate studio, which may lead to them trusting you with larger commissions.

Another way of lowering the costs incurred in renting a studio is to share one with other designers, or like-minded colleagues, on an equal footing. Working with other people is as difficult as living with other people, so think carefully about whom you share with – even if you are friends – and discuss any areas of possible discontent beforehand. You cannot expect colleagues to always fit into your plans – they may like a radio on while they work and you may prefer silence; they may be very tidy and you may not be. Look at fairly basic considerations like these before deciding to work together. Sometimes working with one or more colleagues means you can offer a wider range of complementary skills to customers, and working with illustrators or photographers can be of mutual benefit. Beware of working with direct competitors, unless you are both able to cope with one of you being busy while the other is not.

Another way of sharing the responsibilities of a design business is to form a partnership. This type of association is fraught with difficulties and should be considered very carefully. Do you offer each other benefits and different skills, and are you both going to inject equal effort into making the practice succeed. Remember that a partnership, like any relationship, will only flourish when aims and objectives are clarified and the direction of both partners remains the same. If you decide to go ahead, put an agreement in writing, whatever your relationship is, and make it legal. Partnerships only need this type of agreement if and when the association ends, but that is the very time when an agreement would make a difficult split easier.

The life of a freelancer can seem very glamorous, but it has many pitfalls. It can be demanding in terms of time, because you have to look for, and find, work. Sometimes you may be short of work, at others, you may be hard pressed to meet deadlines. This is because you are entirely dependent on clients for your livelihood. It is untrue to say that a freelancer's life is more independent. It is important, however, that you learn basic business skills so that you can keep accounts, send letters and keep the business running smoothly.

GETTING WORK

The easiest element of working as a freelancer is actually doing the work once you have it. A client who is paying you money naturally expects you to give a good service. This will mean being available for meetings, talking through your ideas and basically keeping them happy. Much of your energy will go into becoming your own public relations officer. You must win the confidence of your client.

But how do you meet clients initially? Whom do you contact? The best form of introduction is recommendation. If you have worked successfully with one customer, they are likely to tell others about you, and so your reputation will grow. The reverse is also true, so remember this before you are late with a job or let anybody down. Success depends on your professional reputation.

Recommendation will come later in your career. Initially, contacts will be made by phoning people up, writing to them, then showing them your portfolio. This can be an extremely disheartening process at first, so brace yourself for the realization that it is not only very difficult to locate potential customers, but also you are going to have lots of refusals. Making contact with a company's marketing team on the telephone can be a major task, let alone persuading them to see your portfolio. You will learn to become persistent – skill in graphics does not qualify you in selling. This is something to consider before you decide on freelancing. Even when you are busy, make time to see new people, because there is no point in being hectic with work one week and then finding yourself unemployed the next. Planning plays a major role in the successful control of your workload.

It is good policy to busy yourself seeing people, even if there are no immediate results. Art directors do keep records, and may contact you several months, even a year, later – you can never tell. But you can be certain that if you do not make the effort to see potential clients, they will never contact you.

If you have already worked in one area of graphics, such as publishing, then that is the obvious starting point in your search for work.

Draw up a list of all the publishers it is practical to visit. Business directories in the public library will give you a company's address, telephone number and a little general information. It will help you judge a company's size and possible design requirements. It is essential when writing to a company that you find out the name of the person to whom your letter should go. This can be found in a directory or by telephoning the company's switchboard and asking. If you have any problem, explain your purpose. Your local business telephone directory will help as well. Try to be logical about who you see, and when you speak to people on the telephone, assess their design requirements and the likelihood of them needing designers – otherwise you may be wasting each other's time. Having said this, the most unlikely sources can often yield an unimaginable quality and quantity of work. So it really is down to trial and error and persistence. If your work is good you will find a market.

THE DESIGN BRIEF

Commercial graphic design always begins with a design brief. A graphic designer should be capable of interpreting and understanding a client's needs. This is sometimes difficult because a client may not know exactly what they want themselves. This is precisely why an initial brief is important – it should be an opportunity to discuss and identify the client's objectives.

A design brief can vary tremendously – it may be a short telephone conversation or a highly detailed typed brief. You may be dealing with people who understand design and its language, or people who know they need something but not always what, are wary of designers and don't really want to spend money on design anyway. Whatever the situation, it is your job to clarify the task and put your client at ease.

Be prepared when you go to a briefing. If you are meeting somebody for the first time, find out a little information about their company beforehand so that you appear well informed. It is important to inspire the client with confidence, and first impressions do count. Take along your portfolio, too.

When you decide on freelancing from home, plan the position and layout of the studio very carefully. Remember that clients will be visiting, so try and separate it as much as possible from the rest of the house.

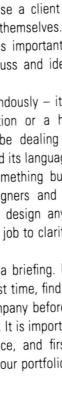

Practical flooring / Light box / Work surface / Comfortable seat for resting and for clients

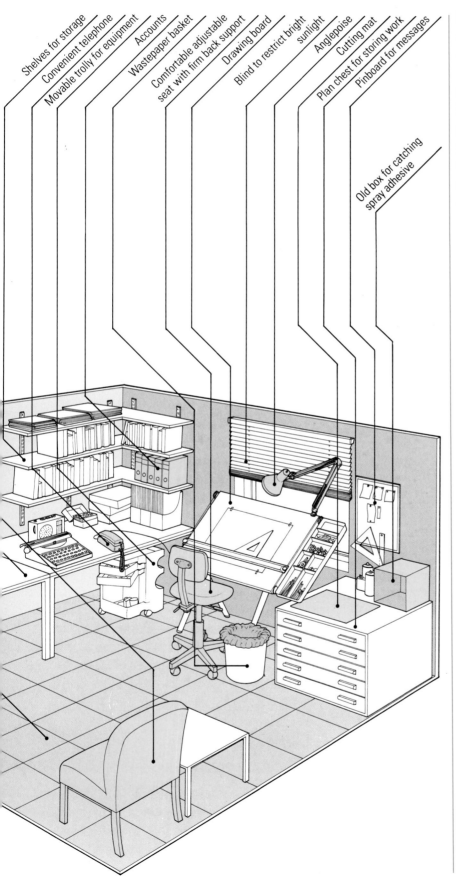

Shelves for storage

Convenient telephone

Movable trolly for equipment

Accounts

Wastepaper basket

Comfortable adjustable seat with firm back support

Drawing board

Blind to restrict bright sunlight

Anglepoise

Cutting mat

Plan chest for storing work

Pinboard for messages

Old box for catching spray adhesive

Bear in mind that your client may not be familiar with technical language so keep the explanation of your ideas quite straightforward.

Assess the job carefully and accurately. Make sure that you fully understand the market the work is aimed at, so your design work is neither too sophisticated nor too down-market to communicate effectively. If you have any real doubts about your ability to cope with the work or finish it as scheduled – allowing time for changes to visuals – discuss them at this point, and if necessary decide not to accept the commission, rather than let the client down later. Try to build in some extra time to allow for the unexpected. It is also helpful to know the names and telephone numbers of anyone else involved in the job, such as authors or production managers, so if you have specific questions you know whom to contact.

Once you have agreed on the design brief you must agree on the budget and confirm it in writing. A client will either expect you to work within a pre-determined budget, or they will ask you to supply an estimate of your charges and costs. You may have to buy services from photographers, printers or illustrators, so always establish these costs before you commit yourself, and unless there are very good reasons to the contrary, stick to them. If for any external reasons a job begins to become more expensive and there are legitimate expenses which you feel your client should pay, let them know immediately.

COSTING TIME

To remain in business, you must be profitable. This applies whether you are a freelancer or running a studio which employs other people. You should base your fees on an hourly rate which takes into account all your overheads. To achieve this hourly figure, total your annual expenses, work out a notional salary for yourself, add these up, and then increase that amount to cover times when you may not be working. Some of your time, for example, will be spent doing administration, which you cannot charge to any one client.

Designers are frequently asked to negotiate a fee. When doing this, aim to make a profit and yet

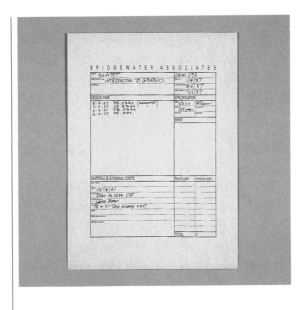

LEFT A job bag system keeps all the information for each job together. In addition, if you allocate each new job a job number, this becomes the invoice number as well and will make your records more efficient.

RIGHT This flow chart shows all the stages of the design process. The briefing session between designer and client is of paramount importance since it is there that the concept of the project is discussed and defined. The designer's task is then to produce the job to the demands of the brief, on time and on budget.

remain competitive. It is important to remember that although design should always be viewed aesthetically, it is also a commodity which is bought and sold, like any other. Your prices must reflect the market rate. New clients need to be won, so you may have to accept a smaller profit on the early work you do for them. You must always be flexible with estimates, otherwise you can find yourself with no clients at all.

To do good business, you must organize and document each job carefully. This does not mean becoming a slave to paperwork, it simply means keeping accurate accounts of all time, meetings, expenses and materials relating to a particular job. This is essential so you are not only in a position to check that you are giving realistic estimates for work, but your invoicing of particular expenses will be much easier. If you do not have a logical system of keeping records, you will easily lose track of time and materials used – especially if several people are working together – and clients will not be charged for the full cost of a job.

A good solution is to create a job bag system. The job bag carries a job sheet, which can either be stuck or printed onto a large envelope. The envelope becomes a file for keeping all correspondence, photographs, small pieces of artwork, notes etc., relating to that job. The job sheet itself is used for recording all time, materials and services, such as typesetting and photographic costs. This method keeps everything in one file.

INVOICING

When you agree budgets and costs with a client, you should also outline your own terms of business. Cash flow is a major problem for companies of all sizes, but in particular for individuals trading on their own. Graphic design is an industry that works at speed – clients often want every job yesterday. To trade successfully, you need to invoice promptly and then ensure that your clients pay you on time. If substantial sums of money are involved, you should ask for an advance.

Be straightforward when discussing terms of business and be wary if you are dealing with a client for the first time. The criteria for payments will depend on how long the job takes, and how much money you will have to pay out for typesetting, photography or other services. If you are particularly concerned, ask for a trade reference, and ask the client to agree terms in writing. On very large commissions you should agree stage payments – say three separate instalments; the first to be paid at the beginning of a job, the second on approval of the design, and the final instalment on completion of the job.

Invoicing when the work is completed is the most common method. Always itemize your invoice clearly, and if necessary enclose a separate sheet of expenses. If you are not paid on time, phone your client and find out why. Be persistent in chasing invoices otherwise you will easily run into financial difficulties.

However busy you are with work, it must never be at the expense of your administration. You must find time to invoice regularly, otherwise, whatever your system, it will be more difficult to calculate costs.

ILLUSTRATORS & PHOTOGRAPHERS

Photographers and illustrators are usually self-employed and often specialize in one particular subject area or style. This is very important to remember when commissioning work. Decide on the type of imagery you would like to use –

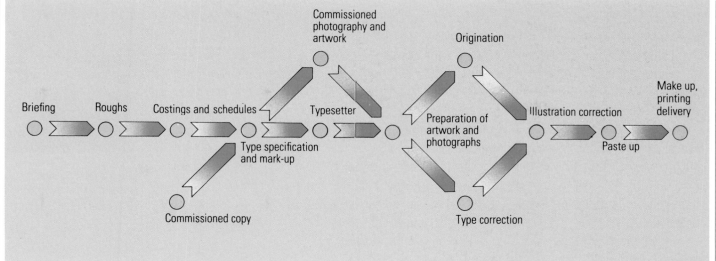

Briefing　Roughs　Costings and schedules　Type specification and mark-up　Commissioned copy　Commissioned photography and artwork　Typesetter　Preparation of artwork and photographs　Type correction　Origination　Illustration correction　Paste up　Make up, printing delivery

decorative, diagrammatic, slick, imaginary, moody, – and whether it should be in colour or black and white, then go to the right photographer or illustrator.

When you intend to commission work it is always important to show the client examples of the style of image you intend to use – especially if it is illustrative work. When you present visuals, give the matter thought and go to the meeting armed with relevant samples. Clients often find photography more acceptable and perhaps easier to understand visually, but both disciplines are essential tools to a designer, and each lends different qualities to a job. Learn to use both to maximum effect.

Choosing and briefing the right person for a commission is difficult, but becomes easier with practice. Both skills are expensive to buy, so it is important to choose individuals whose styles are right for the job, rather than asking them to produce work in styles that are unfamiliar to them. Shrewd designers are always prepared to look at portfolios of work from freelancers, to keep them in touch with different types of work and the prices people are charging. Cost is always a consideration when buying work and must be balanced against quality.

However busy you are when briefing others, it is a false economy to hurry. A hurried brief can cost you dearly when work arrives in the wrong size, or is inappropriate to your needs.

DESIGN

It is important at the outset of a job to clarify and agree the following with your supplier:
■ *The brief*
■ *A schedule of work*
■ *How you want the work to be presented.*
■ *Whether you want to see roughs.*
■ *Are you going to direct the photography?*
■ *Rejection fees*
■ *The finished work will remain in the possession of the illustrator unless you make it clear at the outset that you are buying the original. The illustrator will also retain copyright and this can cause problems if the artwork is re-used.*

T I P

PHOTOGRAPHERS

Photographers normally charge their time by the day, and rates vary depending on the premises and skills they offer. The daily rate does not usually include materials and any other extra expenses, so remember to get an estimate of these before a job begins.

If the job involves working with models or children, make sure that the photographer has the social ability to deal with the situation and also the facilities for the required shot. Always discuss the job thoroughly and agree on how much the work is going to cost. Remember that fees are negotiable, so if you want a particular photographer but your budget cannot accommodate him, be forthright and see if he will do the job for what you can afford. Most photographers are flexible and will lower their rates if they are gaining several days' work. Sometimes they can slot the job into a schedule to suit them which makes it economically viable.

If the job involves models, then you should make the ultimate decision who to use. Photographers often have models they like working with, who are relaxed in front of the camera, so although you should be guided by them, do not automatically assume that whoever they pick will be right.

When you begin to do the art direction during photographic sessions, you may feel inhibited. This may be because you have not worked with the photographer before, and do not feel confident to judge what the result will be like. Take advice from the photographer but be firm in achieving the results that *you* want. You will, of course, find it easier as you gain experience and work with people you know.

When you book time with a photographer arrange for the studio to be ready when you arrive, so that you do not have to wait while equipment is being set up. You may also need to employ a stylist who will organize the delivery of any props needed well in advance.

Always specify whether you want prints or transparencies, what format is required and whether you want alternative shots, so you have a choice of pictures. When the pictures arrive, take great care of them. They will have cost lots of money, so before you accept them examine every detail.

PICTURE LIBRARIES

Photographs can also be borrowed from a picture library or agency. It is easier and cheaper to use a picture from a library than to commission afresh but it may not always be possible. Many libraries hold the work of particular photographers and some specialize in particular subjects; but most libraries have a general collection catalogued by subject matter.

The best way to use a picture library is to make an appointment to visit, having first specified exactly what you are looking for. They will have a selection of photographs ready for you when you arrive, and someone will help you if you need it. You can do all this by telephone and post, but you may specify a particular subject and eventually find what you are looking for in another category, so it is better to go and look for yourself. If the library does all the work you will pay a fairly nominal fee for the service.

The agency loaning the pictures will want to know in what form and size the picture is being used, and in what countries the book, or magazine, is being published so that a reproduction fee can be calculated. They will also want to know the print run – that is, how many books are being printed. The fee is usually payable on publication and pictures should be returned as quickly as possible, otherwise a holding fee may also be charged. Reproduction fees vary from library to library, so before you use a picture make sure you have agreed terms.

Before you borrow pictures, check them very carefully; if they are already damaged and you don't make this clear, you may be charged a replacement fee, and this can be expensive. Check for quality too. It is quite usual to be supplied with duplicate transparencies which are never as sharp as the originals.

ABOVE Picture libraries usually file their collection by subject matter.

BELOW Some pictures cannot be re-commissioned so you are paying for their uniqueness. Picture libraries are often the quickest and most economical source for certain pictures.

ILLUSTRATION

There are almost as many styles of illustration as there are illustrators. Each style adds a different quality to a commission, but being so subjective means that you must be sure about the function you want the illustration to perform. Clients, who perhaps are not used to looking at illustrations may have particular preferences for style. There are many illustrators' annuals available, and this is not only a good way of showing a range of styles to a client, but also a means of choosing one for the job in hand.

Establish a fee with the illustrator at the beginning of a commission. Illustrators usually estimate a job based on their own individual hourly rate, so prices can vary tremendously. You should also

ABOVE AND RIGHT When commissioning a photograph or illustration be certain of what you want to achieve. A subject can be tackled in many different ways and to many different effects. 'Eggs' demonstrates how different the results can be.

establish a rejection fee in case the work is not acceptable. The illustrator will need a full brief, including details of size, colours, overlays etc. and deadlines for each stage of the job, allowing time for alterations.

There are other technical points to consider, too. Sometimes illustrators want their work reproduced at a particular size in order to enhance its style and character, so agree with the illustrator what size they should do the work, to achieve the best results. At the same time, make sure that the illustrators you work with understand the mechanics of working in proportion, especially if they are fresh from college.

It is always a good policy to look at roughs of a job before finished artwork is produced. It ensures that both the designer and illustrator are thinking along the same lines and that the brief is being fulfilled. This is also the last opportunity for you to check with your printer if they require the work on a flexible surface so that it can be scanned.

Finally, remember to give illustrators sufficient copies of the printed job. They have a living to make as well, and their livelihoods depend on their portfolios, just as yours does.

THE DESIGN STUDIO

The design studio is where most graphic designers begin their careers. Studios vary tremendously. They can consist of any number of designers and work in specific design areas, such as three-dimensional display and corporate identity, or they can be totally non-specialist and tackle anything. This diversity means that there is no typical studio but you can be certain that when you work for a busy studio you will work in a highly pressured environment. However, the essence of a successful studio must be design ability and reliability.

Most studios have senior designers who produce designs from a given brief. The brief may come directly from the client or via the art director or account executive. Senior designers will usually have assistants, such as typographers and art-workers, who help produce the work. In other studios which are not so departmentalized, the work is spread more generally. As a junior in a studio

you will be expected to do what might seem like quite menial tasks at first. However, this early experience is essential to your development, and I would strongly recommend that you absorb as much information from those around you as possible.

The pressure in a studio – assuming it is run efficiently – is due to the fact that design and production are final links in an often long chain of people. When clients decide to promote their products, for example, they will invariably be working towards a deadline. Sometimes the deadline is self-imposed, but more often it is a press date, or an exhibition opening – something which happens on a specific day. If any time is lost in the schedule of events before the job reaches the design studio, then that time has to be made up by the design team. This creates the pressure, and, of course, the stimulation and excitement.

The full-time design members of a small general design studio might include the art director, a very experienced senior designer, a designer, a general assistant and a junior. The different roles are, to some degree, interchangeable, especially when more hands are needed to get the work done on time. This sort of studio would have the back-up support of freelancers, including perhaps one regular designer who might work in-house for part of the week, depending on the workload, and others from whom work would be commissioned as and when the need arose. Many studios do most of their own artwork because, it gives control and continuity in the design process right through to the artwork stage. Slight adjustments and refinements which could not be expected of anyone else can then be done more easily.

The art director is usually responsible for dealing with clients and, in turn, briefs the designers. This gives the art director a first-hand insight into each brief and an opportunity to assess the client's exact requirements. It also inspires confidence in the clients, because they know that the art director is directly involved. If the art director is not designing the initial visuals one of the team will be briefed, and then the two of them will probably work closely throughout all stages of the job's development. The art director is ultimately responsible for every job which leaves the studio.

ADVERTISING

An advertisement or promotion is produced on behalf of the advertisers by advertising agencies. This organized industry carries out market research within social groups, on spending power and consumer trends, then directs and organizes a campaign for a client, controlling its exposure through the media. Graphic design is an integral part of all advertising, and the advertising industry is one of the largest sources of work for designers.

The growth of the advertising industry over the last 100 years or so, has been considerable. It plays a vital role in the era of mass production and mass consumption and has become an accepted part of modern life. Without advertising, many products would simply not exist. Industry has to involve itself in mass retailing in order to sell what it makes. It is very difficult to judge the success of advertising in helping to sell a product, because sales also depend on other elements such as product quality, availability, distribution, competition, fashion, and of course, price.

Many people say that advertising adds to the price of a product, but it can be argued that advertising keeps prices lower by stimulating competition. Customers also benefit by having a much wider choice of brands. Advertising is now seen as an essential part of a company's capital investment in its product, and most companies advertise in one form or another.

When a company decides to promote a product or service, it will appoint an agency. Different agencies will usually compete or 'pitch' for the same account, although this is becoming less fashionable. 'Pitching' is usually speculative and involves convincing the client that one particular approach or another will succeed. An agency's experience in a certain area will sometimes be the deciding factor, or perhaps its known ability to handle a very big account efficiently. A large company may decide either to split its products between several agencies, or split the types of advertising, placing say, the press advertising with one agency and the television advertising with another. The company will not want to advertise one brand at the expense of another and this will also affect any decision to use several agencies. It is pointless merely switching sales without developing new customers.

It is important to point out at this stage that not all companies are Ford Motors, nor are all agencies Saatchi and Saatchi. Many highly creative and effective advertisements are produced by small agencies for small companies on low budgets. No two agencies are identical in their structure and organization. Top agencies can offer a total service to their clients, but there are many other agencies and graphic design companies who

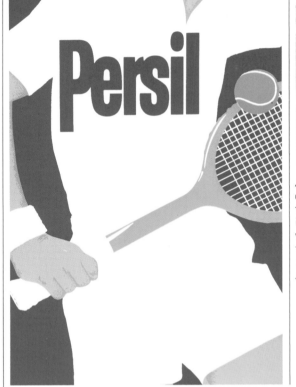

ABOVE This stylish Persil poster shows how eye-catching and visible an image can be.
Agency: J Walter Thompson

ABOVE The Marlboro campaign has been running for 30 years and is now seen in most countries of the world; it has made the brand the largest selling cigarette in the world.
Agency: Leo Burnett

ABOVE Comedy is used very effectively in a series of advertisements for Holsten Pils lager. Comedian Griff Rhys-Jones appears in situations with Hollywood stars and their success depends on the brilliant marrying of old and new film footage.
Agency: Gold Greenlees Trott

offer a partial service and buy outside skills as a back-up.

Many graphic design companies will be asked to produce the occasional press advertisement and perhaps even organize its appearance in a paper or magazine, but they are fundamentally different from advertising agencies. The role of an agency is much more complex. A large agency will have the resources to develop marketing strategies, do market research, provide consumer information, administer the account, analyze audience data and schedule the campaign.

Once an agency has been appointed, it will be given an overall budget, which it has to decide how to utilize to the greatest advantage of the client. An advertising agency makes its money by charging its client 15% of the money it spends on their behalf. This commission is usually paid back to the agency by the media in which the advertising is placed. This percentage varies and like most things is negotiable.

Choosing which media to advertise in will depend on the product, the target audience and the advertising budget. The main areas to choose from are newspapers, magazines, television, radio, posters and direct mail. Once the target audience has been identified the advertising strategy can be planned accordingly. For instance, the target audience for soap powder is unlikely to be the same as that for office equipment. Different advertisers want to reach different audiences, and it is important to know the characteristics of that audience – age, sex, class, income, purchasing habits, and so on. The product can then be exposed through the medium which the agency believes will be most effective.

HEINEKEN REFRESHES THE PARTIES OTHER BEERS CANNOT REACH.

TOP Newspapers are heavily sectionalized and this enables advertisers to place their advertisements in the most appropriate section for their audience.

ABOVE Press advertisements make their point with both words and pictures. In this Heineken press ad the only copy is the long running line "Heineken refreshes the parts other beers cannot reach", and the picture has to do all the work.
Agency: Lowe & Howard-Spink Campbell-Ewald

Once all the planning is done and the information collated, the agency begins to generate the creative ideas which will achieve the client's marketing objectives. The creative team usually comprises a copywriter and an art director. The responsibility for the creative approach lies jointly with these two people, although it is usual for copywriters to head the team.

Once the ideas are agreed, they are presented to the client. The campaign strategy is then planned in cooperation with the media team. They decide on the best use of the budget. Obviously the budget is one of the main criteria for deciding where to advertise. Advertising on television and in national newspapers is expensive so those options might be ruled out immediately in some cases. An advertiser may have specific regional requirements because their market-place is limited to one area of the country. This has to be considered when planning a campaign too.

Once the campaign has run its course, the results have to be measured. This is done by market research. By sampling the responses of a small number of people it is theoretically possible to determine the responses of a much larger group. Market research gauges – as accurately as it can – whether the advertised product or service was right, whether the campaign achieved its objectives and whether better results can be achieved next time.

PUBLISHING

Publishing, broadly speaking, covers the production, distribution and marketing of books and magazines. Magazines are published regularly and need a loyal audience to survive. The launch of a new magazine involves much planning, market research and testing in order to predict whether it is likely to be a success or not. Sales figures influence advertisers and advertising revenue can be a vital source of revenue. The higher a magazine's circulation the more expensive the advertising rates may be. Conversely, a magazine with a shrinking circulation begins to lose advertising.

The first stage of preparing a new magazine is to produce a prototype or 'dummy'. This is simply a very glossy, highly finished mock-up of the cover and several inside pages. This is shown to potential advertisers to test their reactions. While the magazine is being conceived, dummies will be produced many times over in order to define the style of the publication and create a format with which everybody is happy. This is a tremendously exciting and satisfying process for a designer to be involved in. Once the magazine is launched, the style will continue to develop issue by issue, with the advertising, editorial and design departments working closely together to improve the appeal of their product and react to public feedback.

Magazine advertising is pre-sold and often the position of an ad is decided long before an issue is designed. The designer will usually have no control over the look of advertisements – because they are supplied by the companies advertising their products or by their agencies. This also affects the editorial content of the magazine.

BOOK PUBLISHING

The high level of competition between publishers has totally changed the traditional approach to publishing. Although ideas and manuscripts still arrive unsolicited from hopeful authors, some of which become books, publishing programmes are now planned carefully.

Book production and marketing are expensive operations and books rarely attract advertising or advertising revenue. In fact, most books are totally financed by the number of copies sold. Occasionally a book will have a sponsor who helps finance its production. The sponsor's name may even help to sell the book.

Unless the author is well established or a celebrity the cover is the main selling device. It must be strong enough visually to compete with all the other books on the shelf. Gaining approval for a cover design is often a lengthy process, involving the sales and marketing divisions of a company. Designers often find it difficult to accept cover designs virtually imposed on them by sales staff.

Illustrated books offer further design challenges. Illustrated book publishing is particularly expensive and it is now unusual to produce a

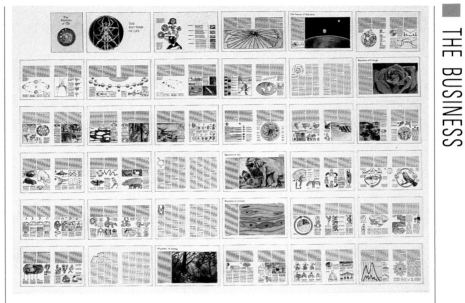

ABOVE Flow charts are miniature layouts that enable a designer to see a book as a whole and plan where pictures and colour should fall.

lavish book without first selling publishing rights to foreign publishers and book clubs. By increasing the number of copies printed in the original print run, the manufacturing price per copy is reduced. When a book is produced for different markets and countries it is called a 'co-edition'.

A fairly new but rapidly growing innovation in book production is the book packager. A book packager does not publish or distribute books, but sells rights and then produces the book for the publisher at a negotiated price. This can sometimes be much more cost-effective for the publisher as well as cutting out the attendant administrative problems of dealing with authors, designers, photographers and other suppliers.

Many of today's more lavish books are the work of packagers. The packagers conceive the original idea, produce a sales dummy which will be used to sell the rights to different publishers around the world, and then produce the book in its different editions. They will supply either finished, bound copies, or in some cases just the film so the publisher can organize the printing.

Well-planned co-edition publishing involves producing books for several different clients at the same time. The most expensive elements in illustrated book production are usually the costs of colour separation and printing. When anything is printed, the greater the quantity the lower the individual unit cost. This is because there are certain fixed costs, however large the print quantity. The text for each language can be over-printed once the illustrations have been printed.

Many books are conceived and designed well before any words are ever written. Working from a synopsis, a designer will produce a 'flow-chart', or 'flat-plan', which is simply a miniature layout. It enables the book to be seen as a whole and is ideal for juggling around with the content and for planning where the pages of colour will fall, for example. For economic reasons colour will not necessarily be available on all pages, and so it is important to use the colour availability well. When there is a *very* limited number of colour pages in a book or magazine, or when the colour is printed on a different paper from the text, the pages can be incorporated as a single section, or as 'wraps' and 'inserts'. This means wrapping or inserting four or more pages around the outside of, or into a text section. This is an effective method of spreading colour evenly through a book, and actually creates an illusion of there being more colour than there actually is.

MAGAZINE & BOOK PRODUCTION

■ Initial roughs of styling for discussion.
■ Produce finished 'dummy' presentation or 'flow-chart' for sales purposes.
■ Agree production specifications.
■ Design and finalize jacket or cover – this is always one of the first things to be done, so it can be used to help sell the book or magazine.
■ Draw up the grid artwork and get grid sheets printed. Order one quantity on tracing paper for layout purposes, and another on artboard for the final camera-ready paste-up of the text.
■ Mark up the edited manuscript and send for typesetting.
■ Plan any commissioned illustration and photography as early as possible. Sometimes this can only be done after the layout is complete, but if you know this will be required, decide who to commission and book their time.
■ Galley proofs returned from the typesetter. One

set will come to you for laying the book out, and others will go to the editor and author for checking.
■ Paste down the galleys onto the tracing paper grids and finalize the picture areas.
■ Once the required 'extent', or number of pages, has been successfully filled, pictures can be traced into their areas and any copy amendments needed in order for the text to fit precisely can be marked.
■ Layouts are sent to the editor for checking and writing captions. Caption positions should always be marked on the layouts so that directions such as 'above' or 'opposite' can be included in the caption if necessary.
■ Layouts, captions and edited galley proofs are returned to the designer.
■ Typographic style changes are marked on the edited set of galleys, the captions are marked up by the designer and returned to the typesetter. 'Folios', or page numbers, running-heads, contents, etc. must have been marked up for setting.
■ A photocopy of the layout can be sent to an indexer at this stage. Indexing is a specialized skill and requires the listing of all significant subjects and names and the page numbers they fall on.
■ Final galley proofs are returned. Again, one set goes to the editor for checking, and another to the designer for camera-ready paste-up.
■ The galley of the text is pasted onto the artboard grids, along with any black and white artwork.
■ Once this is done, the galleys on the tracing layouts can be removed. The tracing layouts – which have all the picture positions traced on them – can then be attached to the artboard as an overlay. This not only protects the artwork, but shows the size and position of the pictures in relation to the text.
■ The book can then be marked up for the colour reproduction house or printer. This should be done on the tracing grid overlay.
■ The book is now ready to go for colour separation. Check everything thoroughly.
■ Any last minute line changes in text can be pasted in as individual lines, called 'line strips'.
■ The responsibilities of the designer extend to checking the colour proofs.

TOP RIGHT Product packaging can be purely functional or, as in this Crabtree & Evelyn design, so beautiful that it is desirable in itself.

BOTTOM RIGHT Record sleeves are produced to various standard formats and designers therefore have to work particularly hard using fashion and applied graphics to sell the product.

PACKAGING

Packaging a product is another specialist area of the design industry, and few graphic design studios have the real expertise to deal with the process fully. The designer's task when dealing with packaging is to produce an effective selling device.

The pack itself is often the only element of the product on display for shoppers to see, and the design is the only way that manufacturers can communicate their ideas to the customer. Packaging can serve as purely functional wrapping, or it can be attractive enough in itself to tempt the purchaser. Packaging can shout loudly, and, in its most prestigious form, totally seduce.

A can of oil and a box of cereal do not have to look the way they do – they have been designed. New packaging approaches are continually sought for long established products. Packaging can also make a product easier to transport, more practical to display, and more convenient to use.

Packaging has developed alongside mass production and the evolution of retail selling. Supermarkets are designed for shoppers to select items themselves, without the help of assistants, and the range of products on the shelves are packaged to sell themselves. The shopper often depends on the pack to reveal its contents. The pack not only creates brand identity and appeal but has to fulfil statutory requirements such as listing accurate details of contents, quantities and nutritional values.

Manufacturers readily appreciate the selling power of good package design and consistently invest time and money in this sophisticated market. The designer cannot control how a package will be handled or displayed once it has left the manufacturer, but must take these aspects into account in the design. A pack is a three-dimensional object which is handled. It is placed alongside competing packages for the shopper to choose, it may be viewed from several angles and it should be bought by the customer. The packaging designer must be concerned with the graphics and also the details of the material, its construction, sealing and manufacture.

89

Superficially, graphic design for television resembles graphic design for print. The image is two-dimensional and its composition — a grid of coloured dots — resembles a printed image created using a half-tone screen. However, that collection of electronically activated dots offers the graphic designer opportunities which are unique.

Consider the infinite permutations of design possible using photographic, illustrative and abstract ingredients of form, line and texture. Then multiply these permutations by the infinite variations of movement, light and sound.

All media impose technical constraints or have characteristics which will influence the conception and execution of a project. Happily, the technology of television is so advanced that such constraints are few. The format of the screen is a 4:3 ratio and this is, of course, fixed. Apart from a need to avoid excessively saturated colours or type forms which are too small or fragile in their design, television will cope with virtually any kind of image. The only limitations are those faced in any commercially controlled medium: time, money, talent.

Transmitted television is the end product of a very sophisticated technology. There is a tendency to regard the graphic designers working in television either as artistic boffins, or to assume that a knowledge of advanced imaging systems is essential before they can tackle the creative aspect of the job. Familiarity with the technical aspects of production will obviously improve designers' confidence in the medium, but the quality of the televised graphic image will depend ultimately on design talent.

How does the design get from the drawing board onto the screen? At the most primitive level, a caption card can be placed in front of a video camera. At the most advanced level it can mean a lengthy, expensive process involving powerful computers or a whole film studio.

Movement is the magic ingredient which separates television graphics from its print-based counterparts. At the primitive caption-card level, movement can be applied at the control desk by a vision mixer or video editor. At the touch of a

ABOVE Perhaps the most successful advertising music of all time was the song 'I'd like to buy the world a coke' from the 1971 Coca-Cola 'Hilltop' commercial, which became a world-wide hit as 'I'd like to teach the world to sing'. After that, every advertiser wanted to have a No. 1 hit. *Agency: McCann-Erickson.*

button, zooms, wipes, fades and flip-overs, can be activated. Ideally these should be controlled by the graphic designer, but for practical reasons they are often controlled by the editor, director or producer. This accounts, to some extent, for the predictable character of such instant effects. Only when a designer is given total responsibility for a whole sequence can the style, movement and sequential structure of the graphics be fully controlled.

Although film technology is increasingly giving ground to videotape, its distinctive character and accessibility at the editing stage will guarantee its use for some time. The film set-up most commonly used by graphic designers involves a 35mm or 16mm movie camera designed, or adapted, to expose single frames. It is mounted to shoot and move vertically at right angles to a table carrying the artwork. This table is also capable of lateral and rotational movements. The set-up is known as a Rostrum Camera Stand, or an Animation Stand. The combination of these camera and table movements, as well as fades and dissolves, can be controlled to a specific number of frames. Increasingly, such equipment is linked to a computer, giving greater control over the recording of elaborate movements or multiple exposures. Computer-controlled camera effects should not be confused with computer-generated graphics.

In place of the film camera, a Rostrum Stand can hold a video camera. The advantage of being able to record and instantly play back pictures is obvious, but this must be offset against the inability to record multiple superimposed images.

Movement can be built into the artwork itself by creating a series of sequential pictures, that is, by drawn animation. The cartoon animation industry tends to follow methods and styles developed by the American cartoon studios, in particular the work of Walt Disney; but there is a great deal of innovation in the field.

Computer animation, sometimes mistakenly regarded as a threat to traditional cartoon methods, has quite different characteristics and potential. The computer can tirelessly generate series of almost identical images of complex three-dimensional objects, and so it can tackle the movement of such objects in space with a degree of refine-

ment that a human animator would never consider. Unfortunately, flexible articulation of humanoid forms is only possible if a disproportionate amount of data is prepared *for* the computer or if complex, expensive programmes are specially written.

The dimension of movement can also be achieved by the more direct traditional means of filming three-dimensional objects, using methods developed for stop-frame puppet animation or conventional live-action. Any of these techniques can be used exclusively or can be combined at a final editing stage.

The introduction of computers revolutionized not only the means of animation, but also the generating of static individual images. Computer based imaging systems, commonly referred to as electronic paintboxes, were developed for news and current affairs programmes which require graphic material at extremely short notice. Much of this material deals with repeatable or predictable imagery such as maps, charts and stock photographs. The electronic paintbox can be used to call up certain standard pre-recorded pictures and make additions or amendments instantly. The designer 'draws' directly with an electronic pen and can choose from a 'menu' of colours, pen widths, textures, rules and boxes, for example. Smooth gradations of tone — the electronic equivalent of airbrushing — can be achieved

without the skills normally required for airbrush work.

All of these images and combinations are achieved without artwork. Existing pictures can be input from videotape and modified or combined with graphic elements. Considered initially, as a convenient means of imitating conventional artwork, electronically generated pictures have developed a style that has dominated the industry.

Typography, probably the most common graphic element, is not dealt with kindly by television. Unlike print technology, which gives the designer complete control over the final product, electronic typography is modified by the brightness, contrast and colour saturation of the domestic television receiver. Initially, and to some extent today, type is set using traditional metal or photosetting systems and then televised directly by a video camera or scanned from transparencies. The introduction of the character generator has simplified and revolutionized the means of displaying type on the screen. Because each character is composed as a collection of electronic pixels, almost any typeface whatever its weight or character can be generated. Legibility, a factor governed by the 4:3 ratio and a limited display time, remains a major consideration. Similar in operation to a word processor, text correction, character and line-spacing are controlled from a keyboard.

Despite a certain amount of specialization, most designers, working either as freelancers or staff in television companies, find their talents stretched across a wide range of programmes. The versatility demanded of a television graphic designer can be best demonstrated by examining some of the different categories of programme production — News/Current Affairs, drama, light entertainment, educational, promotion and presentation.

The design and production process will obviously vary from project to project but in broad terms this method has a common structure. The designer is briefed, considers the possible solutions, then puts these ideas into some visible form — usually a storyboard — which is presented to the 'client'. If the concept is approved, then the cost of production will be estimated and, once the budget is approved, the project will go into production.

ABOVE The advertising industry has increasingly called on the talents of television graphic designers. Computer-generated graphics provide glossy images, and so 'high tech' graphics frequently feature in commercials. At the other end of the scale, raw, casual innovative animation – often stimulated by art students' experimental work – gives advertisers a link with the valuable youth market.

The electronic paintbox is a computer capable of ammending pre-recorded pictures, creating information graphics, and achieving many other effects without artwork. This new technology is becoming daily more sophisticated, but is only as imaginative as the operator controlling it.

LEFT Brilliant British TV character Max Headroom, created by Annabel Jankel and Rocky Norton, 1985, to be the host of a TV video show. Film frames of the talking head – in fact an actor in Latex make-up – are shuffled and repeated under computer control to give a jerky effect, and the swirling background is computer-generated.

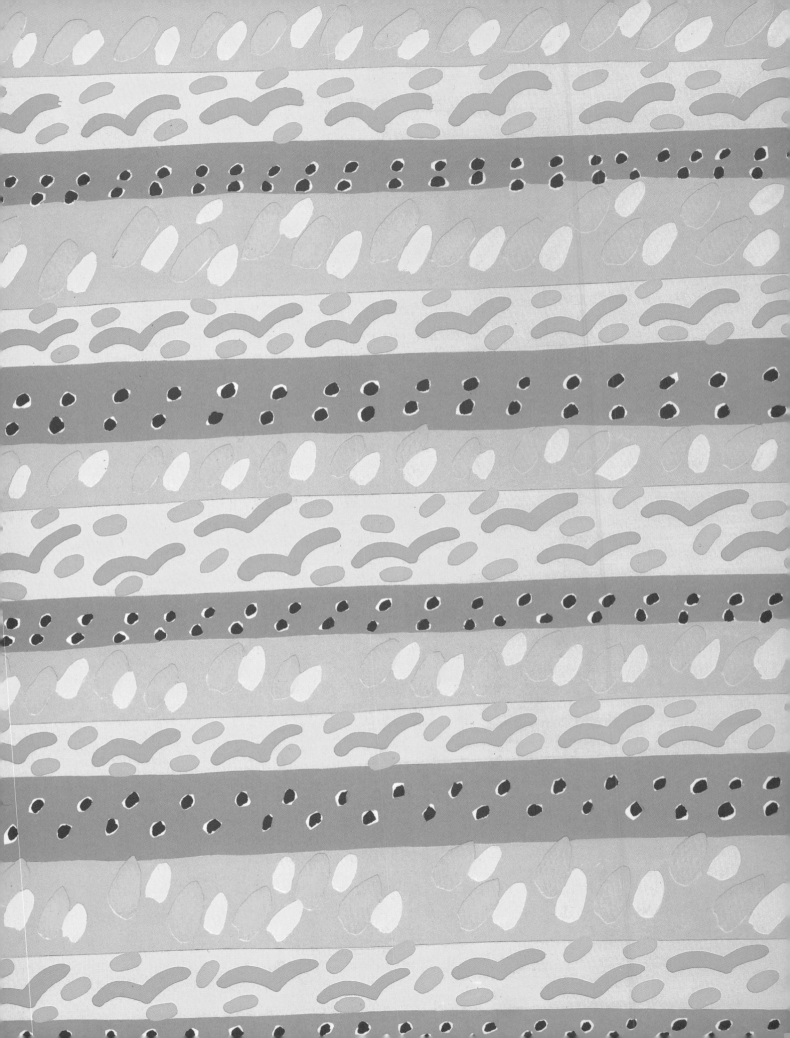

CHAPTER FIVE

DESIGN PORTFOLIO

███ **Patrick Uden, the executive producer of the series, wanted a title sequence with a minimum shelf life of three years. In particular he required a sequence 'charged with mystery and atmosphere', but also something which would be sufficiently general to suit a wide variety of programme material.**

The series was planned to carry all Channel Four's science-based material, with particular emphasis placed on applied science and technology. A title had to be chosen as well.

Various approaches to the brief were considered. Initially an attempt was made to use images relating to individual aspects of science and technology. Some of these images were visually interesting, but a suitable and original vehicle for carrying these images was never successfully developed. The effect of an object encountering different types of surfaces — a metal ball touching glass, rolling or falling into water, meeting rubber or sand, for example — was another idea considered. This approach reflected quite well the 'applied' feel of the series, but technical problems in achieving the desired results discounted it as a viable solution.

At this point it was decided that the series should be called Equinox. It was a title that was too good to ignore. The dictionary definition of the word equinox is: *'The time at which the sun crosses the equator, making day and night equal in length'.* A fundamental basis of all science is the power of the sun and man's reliance on its energy for life itself, so it seemed natural that the alignment of the sun at the point of equinox should be used in some way. The idea of a 'light factory' was developed, whereby a series of mirrors and lenses would be used to divert the sun's energy to create a man-made image. Initially, this image was going to be the logo of the series, or, more specifically, the 'I' of Equinox. There were a lot of points in favour of this idea. The 'I' is the centre character of the word Equinox, suggesting the equator; the characters on either side could then suggest night and day. A logo was developed in which these elements were incorporated. However, it was decided by Patrick Uden that the image was too complicated and eventually the idea of a logo was

CHAPTER FIVE

DESIGN
PORTFOLIO

TITLE SEQUENCE FOR CHANNEL FOUR'S 'EQUINOX'

Patrick Uden, the executive producer of the series, wanted a title sequence with a minimum shelf life of three years. In particular he required a sequence 'charged with mystery and atmosphere', but also something which would be sufficiently general to suit a wide variety of programme material.

The series was planned to carry all Channel Four's science-based material, with particular emphasis placed on applied science and technology. A title had to be chosen as well.

Various approaches to the brief were considered. Initially an attempt was made to use images relating to individual aspects of science and technology. Some of these images were visually interesting, but a suitable and original vehicle for carrying these images was never successfully developed. The effect of an object encountering different types of surfaces — a metal ball touching glass, rolling or falling into water, meeting rubber or sand, for example — was another idea considered. This approach reflected quite well the 'applied' feel of the series, but technical problems in achieving the desired results discounted it as a viable solution.

At this point it was decided that the series should be called Equinox. It was a title that was too good to ignore. The dictionary definition of the word equinox is: *'The time at which the sun crosses the equator, making day and night equal in length'*. A fundamental basis of all science is the power of the sun and man's reliance on its energy for life itself, so it seemed natural that the alignment of the sun at the point of equinox should be used in some way. The idea of a 'light factory' was developed, whereby a series of mirrors and lenses would be used to divert the sun's energy to create a man-made image. Initially, this image was going to be the logo of the series, or, more specifically, the 'I' of Equinox. There were a lot of points in favour of this idea. The 'I' is the centre character of the word Equinox, suggesting the equator; the characters on either side could then suggest night and day. A logo was developed in which these elements were incorporated. However, it was decided by Patrick Uden that the image was too complicated and eventually the idea of a logo was

lack of interesting designs, but because it was felt that using the sun's energy to produce a logo would not be an impressive enough way to end the sequence, and that it would also be predictable.

Some major image had to be created which was both unusual and memorable. A beam of light creating a face which could mouth the word Equinox was the idea which was developed finally. A series of drawings of the individual components of the 'light factory' were produced, together with a diagram of the passage of light produced. These were passed on to Steve Wisher, the model maker. It was essential to the image that the components, while having optical precision, should look as though they were constructed for a factory environment rather than a laboratory. Nuts and bolts and mechanical imperfections were a crucial part of this look.

A low-powered laser gun was used to direct a beam of light through a system of mirrors and lenses. The motion control rig at Moving Picture Company, operated by Peter Truckle, was used over a period of six days to shoot the sequence. Two passes on each part of the sequence were necessary because the laser light itself, while obvious to the eye, did not appear strongly on film. One camera pass exposing for the beam was combined with a second pass with the beam switched off, exposing for ambient light on the model set-up. Various shots of the equipment aligning itself in preparation for the moment of Equinox were taken, and the whole lot put together at a video edit. A face was shot onto videotape mouthing the word equinox to a synthesized voice track. The result was percentage exposed into a spreading beam of light, produced separately using light scan techniques on a film rostrum camera.

Music was commissioned from Dave Vorhaus, whose brief was to use mechanical sounds as far as possible. The whole sequence is 25 seconds long and has just appeared with the first series of 13 programmes on Channel Four.

LEFT The face evolving from a beam of light creates an image which is both mysterious and haunting.

INSETS The 'light factory' which harnessed the sun's energy was specially constructed to appear man-

or broadsheet, to be sent to existing contacts and potential customers. The finished product is to reflect and promote the care, expertise and design excellence that Bridgewater Associates offer as a design group, and to have a life of two years. Size, copy, content and budget unknown.

Promoting yourself can be very difficult indeed as you are both the designer and the client. I was conscious of wanting to produce an aesthetically pleasing and effective result. I also wanted to produce the promotional material as economically as possible, but was determined that it should look and feel good.

The first thing I did was make a conscious decision not to simply show a selection of the work we had already done. Existing clients knew our work and I specifically wanted to show potential customers that we dealt with design in a considered way. I also knew that meeting a contact for the first time meant showing our portfolio, so I wanted this promotion to be a prelude to that. Showing a selection of our work on a small scale was not the way I wanted to introduce ourselves. This promotion would be going to businesses as different as pharmaceuticals and publishing, and it had to be suitably effective for both.

I wanted to suggest, too, that our solutions to a design problem would be more imaginative than those of many other studios, to make a statement of my strong belief in the design team of which I was a part.

When I first set up Bridgewater Associates I had designed a logo which was a visual play on my name. The logo always seemed well received and although I had changed the style of typography on my stationery when I moved office, I had never wanted to change the logo. After playing around with several other ideas I decided to use my existing trademark as the theme of the promotion. This had the additional bonus of impressing my name on new contacts.

Searching through several books, I eventually found the watercolour painting by John Sell Cotman called *Greta Bridge*, painted in 1805, which I had originally used as reference when

Watercolour painting.

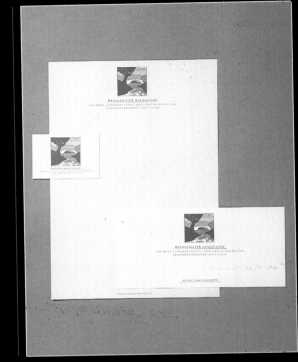

RIGHT The two-colour logo was originally designed for use on stationery.

LEFT AND BELOW The original photographs of the bridge were very disappointing so a different background was laid underneath them in order to enhance the finished result.

LEFT This gouache illustration was designed to reflect the mood and style of 1930's travel posters.

RIGHT As a total contrast this energetic watercolour has a more contemporary look than the gouache.

designing my logo. This was the basis of my decision to show that design is flexible and can be tackled in different ways using different images to different effect.

Once I knew the message I wanted to convey, the layout was done very quickly. I decided to present several other alternatives of the logo including my own treatment in the belief that this would be fun and promote the name Bridgewater very effectively. I commissioned two illustrations from illustrators who I knew would tackle the work in totally different ways.

Then I came to the tricky part. I wanted a moody photograph of the bridge at Greta (if it still existed). I looked through several picture libraries without success and eventually commissioned a photographer to do it.

The results were appalling. Not only was the water low, and the time of the year wrong, but many of the trees around the bridge had been cut down. To overcome these drawbacks I decided to mask out the sky of the commissioned photograph and project a more interesting one into its place. By smearing the lens with petroleum jelly the whole image was softened.

The last task was to decide on the copy. The main headline came to me quite early on, but the selling text itself was a separate problem. I wrote briefly what I wanted to say and gradually reduced it to the essence of what I felt Bridgewater Associates was about.

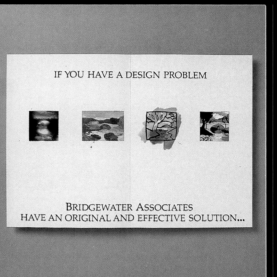

IF YOU HAVE A DESIGN PROBLEM

BRIDGEWATER ASSOCIATES
HAVE AN ORIGINAL AND EFFECTIVE SOLUTION...

LEFT The four images together imply an ability to tackle a design problem in different ways.

BELOW The final brochure was laminated and folded and then sent out with a covering letter.

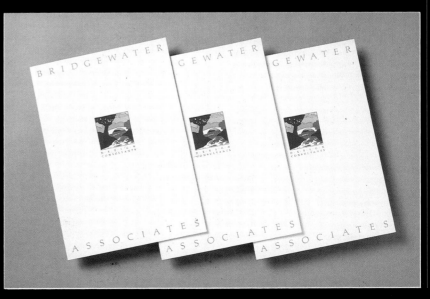

PACKAGING FOR 'CRABTREE & EVELYN'

Crabtree & Evelyn decided that they needed a range of Sun Care products which would have both great cosmetic value and all the normal sun tanning properties.

It was decided that the product should be made in Switzerland to achieve the best possible quality. In designing the packaging, three important aims in the brief had to be achieved:

■ The high quality of the Swiss product had to be conveyed clearly in the packaging design.

■ The products had to be recognized instantly as a Sun Care range.

■ The range was aimed at a young market which was to be reflected in the packaging design without detracting from the overall image of Crabtree & Evelyn products.

The designs went through three or four stages from initial flat roughs, to a three-dimensional dummy carton, to alternative rough illustration and finished packs.

The central image of the palm tree was chosen for its obvious connections with hot sun, sea and sand, but it was treated in a different way to distinguish between the different types of products. The design was also altered within the groups of products so that the more 'serious' products had an appearance which resembled cosmetics. The range was accompanied by beach towels, T-shirts and a counter display unit.

Crabtree & Evelyn have evolved a distinctive style of packaging that reflects tradition and quality.

LEFT The initial ideas were produced flat and a style of illustration established which would appeal to the youth market.

BOTTOM LEFT Three-dimensional dummy packs.

RIGHT AND FAR RIGHT The illustrations were then commissioned from an illustrator and colour roughs presented.

BELOW The finished range retains the Crabtree & Evelyn hallmark of sophistication while creating a more carefree style.

To design a series of advertisements to promote Metro – a chain of large upmarket fashion shops in Singapore. The clothes are expensive, ready to wear and designed primarily for the 20–30 age group.

We began by establishing the project's objectives with our client. This ensured that the design solution we ultimately created reinforced and enhanced the client's marketing strategy. After this initial meeting we began our detailed research into the organization, structure and market of our client's company.

Drawing up questionnaires and group discussion are two of the methods of research we use. Our research was complete once we felt that we knew our client's business inside and out.

We analyzed the information we had gained and discussed this with our client. This was quite an informal meeting, although clients often request a formal presentation of our findings, including exhibits.

We then began work on the design ideas based on the decisions made at the previous meeting. We produced scamps for various proposals to demonstrate the range of possibilities.

We worked through each of our proposals with them, explaining how and why we had arrived at each design. Clients sometimes come to these meetings with very strong preconceived ideas about their own advertising.

We had narrowed down our designs to about two or three which the client liked, and then we worked on the scamps and produced finished visuals. Once we got the go-ahead, we selected models for photography. Lighting and mood are critical and clothes have to be crisp and good-looking. This is the moment when close attention to detail is crucial.

From the contact prints, we selected the best shot and started on the camera-ready artwork. From this stage, the art director supervised the execution of artwork, paying attention to the smallest details, such as spelling, the cropping of photographs, neatness and accuracy. The final job was then approved by the client in time to meet the first copy date.

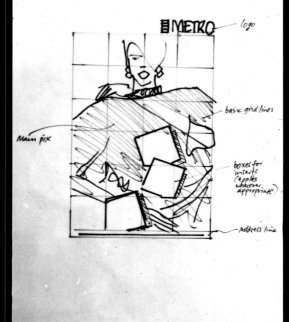

ABOVE The main 'Metro' store in Singapore.

LEFT AND BOTTOM LEFT The initial ideas were produced as black and white marker visuals as the ads were primarily monotone. The grid lines were to run through the entire campaign and the inset boxes were designed to change as necessary.

THIS
LUNAR
NEW
YEAR

Welcome to Metro,
the centre of fabulous
shopping in Singapore.
For souvenirs. Gifts.
The latest fashionwear.
The finest household-
ware. And superb
service that makes you
feel at home.

ABOVE Once the client had
approved the concept,
several models were
selected to enhance the
youthful good-looking appeal
of clothes.

TOP AND RIGHT Black and white
and full-colour versions from
the range of finished ads.

POSTER FOR 'SALUTE'

To design a poster which portrays the style and atmosphere of Salute, an avant-garde clothes shop. The poster is to promote a spring and summer collection using two colours, within a low budget, size unknown. One of the simplest and most direct forms of advertising is a message pasted on a wall. The wall can be a hoarding, the inside of a bus or any site which people can easily see. Poster advertising is a relatively cheap form of promotion, and because posters are on continual display they are seen again and again. Posters placed near supermarkets or busy retail outlets are an excellent reminder medium for advertisers who want to reach buyers about to make their purchases. Poster graphics are usually bold with a main focal point and slogan.

I designed the Salute poster to catch the attention of the passers-by as well as the people who were already in the shop. The poster was planned to enhance rather than dominate the surrounding environment. The appeal was in the abstract corporate identity which is the essence of Salute. I wanted to provide interest and mystery for shoppers, rather than make use of the obvious cliché of a beautiful model projecting sex appeal through clothes. Many of the clothes are unisex and the target-audience consisted of young people with the desire to look stylish.

Salute's approach to marketing has always been low key and individual. The shop has promoted this quality in a tantalizing way from the beginning, and its success is reflected in a growing audience who associate themselves with Salute's aspirations.

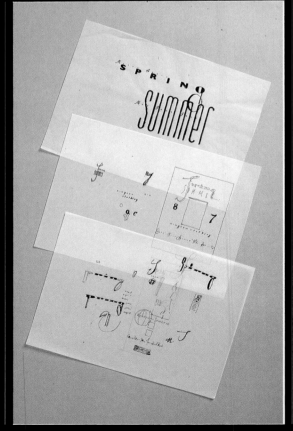

FAR LEFT The original hand lettering logo.

LEFT 'Salute' had always presented a low-key contemporary style to shoppers and the appeal was designed to be mysterious.

RIGHT Hand-lettering and calligraphy played an important role in the design work for Salute. The original ideas were drawn on tracing paper – an ideal surface for working out type design.

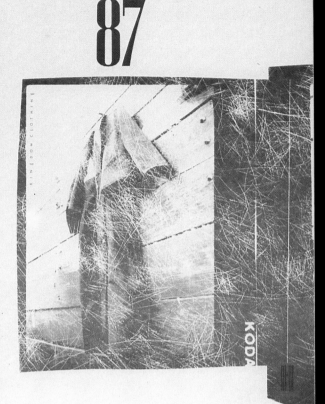

ABOVE Artworking the type is a continual process of re-drawing and refining until the weight and balance of the lettering are right.

RIGHT The finished poster measures 11 x 25 in (28 x 63.5cm).

ABOVE The main image itself was developed by experimenting with different screen PMTs of photographs until the right tantalizing graphic image was produced.

TITLE SEQUENCE FOR 'THE SOUTH BANK SHOW'

I have designed and animated six of these sequences. Melvyn Bragg and I have worked well together over the years, and now we have got to the point where he just lets me get on with the job. We might have a few discussions about who should appear in the titles each time, but he usually leaves this up to me.

I am a graphic designer trained in the 1960s who moved into television graphics at a later stage. This was the moment when I realized that all the techniques and images that I loved in printed graphics could not be applied to screen graphics. This is largely due to what is known as 'cut-off'.

The traditional design aesthetic with all its spatial precision needed an accurately defined frame, so that the elements within it could be read and understood in the most effective way. In television, the cut-off does not allow this. The cut-off is the area around the edge of the screen which gets lost from view and with it goes the control of the design elements within the screen area.

So what *does* work well on television? The answer is movement and sound. To design for the television screen is to have the ability to make things move. This realization threw new light onto the problems of TV design for me.

I have since applied this theory to all my work, and it seems to have worked. The most successful example would be the titles for The South Bank Show.

I very rarely show Melvyn Bragg a storyboard, but, on one occasion, so many different ideas were coming to mind that I thought it would be a good idea to be clear about the finished product. So I prepared the sequence, in rough and in full colour, as an animatic. This is a video tape version showing the key drawings of the sequence in rough, not the full animation, against the music. Afterwards I stuck to this animatic scheme exactly.

The greatest problem I had was finding good reference for the artists who were to appear. I spent ages trying to match good photographs to my list of celebrities, until I eventually gave up and went to the library and raided their file of portraits. I found hundreds of good people that I hadn't considered, so I made a new selection and sat there

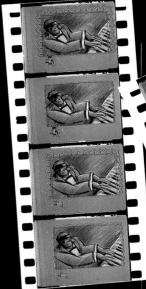

THE FINISHED TITLES. There were things about them that I liked – Ray Charles, James Joyce, the moving cottage, Pete Townsend, Baryshnikov. The part I liked the most was lost on television: the vibrating border which contains all the action disappears because it is too close to the cut-off area.

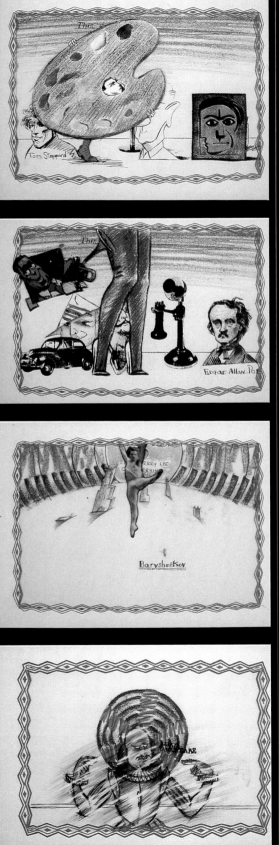

and drew all my caricatures. It took me a day and a half to draw the 40 characters, which then had to be integrated with those faces in the animation. It was obvious that we did not have the time to animate them all, so I selected a few that would be animated. The rest would appear as static drawings.

How were the figures going to move? Should each figure have its own characteristic movements? Were they going to be reacting to something else in the shot, or were they going to start their own piece of action? Walking seemed to be the obvious solution. The music has a good up-tempo march quality, so the figures could march to the music. But all those characters marching around the screen for 30 seconds felt like a lot of work to me in the time we had left. Expediency came to the rescue. Why not make them one character? How? By changing them on every beat, a quick bit of metamorphosis. And that was the scheme I adopted for the animatic.

The first part to be animated was the lettering. In a way this set the style for the whole sequence. We then concentrated on animating the people. Our first attempts seemed very flat, so I changed the drawings to help with the animation. For example, Ray Charles was being a bit difficult because he would not behave as I wanted him to. But Kim, the animator, solved the problem by minimizing his movements.

There are many unforeseen obstacles to overcome in making a sequence like this one. We managed to finish it with time to spare, but then we discovered that nobody liked the end. I think this was because the action had stopped in the last few frames and we were left looking at an illustration, a badly drawn one at that. It was up to me to come up with a final solution. So I turned Shakespeare into an Oscar Schlemmer, Bauhaus figurine in monochrome, gently illuminated by the blue of the spark. Why I went for this I don't really know, but it brings me back to what I was saying earlier about the lack of compatibility between traditional design and the television medium. As much as I have loved cartoon techniques, and the clash, flash and clamour of what has become the style of contemporary TV graphics, I think I am beginning to feel a need for simplicity.

To design a 'teaser' ad for the new Peugeot 309. Its aim is to inform the public that the car is about to be launched and to promote Oval as a dealer. Size: 3 columns wide × 22 cm deep – black and white.

Look through any newspaper and you will see black and white advertisements promoting everything from carpets to cars. They are printed on poor quality, off-white 'newsprint' paper and many reflect an appalling level of design. Some are produced by the newspapers' own advertising departments as part of their service to advertisers, and others are produced by small agencies and graphic design studios. Newspapers which produce the ads as part of their service usually have little incentive to produce successful graphics. Their primary concern is the advertising revenue which is paid to them by the advertiser and they offer a design service in order to help sell the space.

Most press ads for local newspapers are produced on a limited budget and done very quickly. These two elements determine the approach. Small budgets mean you cannot afford a professional copywriter, so often the copy is written by the designer, based on notes supplied by the client. Clarify precisely the elements of your brief:

- ◼ What is the purpose of the ad?
- ◼ Who is the target-audience?
- ◼ What is the deadline?
- ◼ What is the budget?
- ◼ Who is your contact?
- ◼ Is copy supplied or are you organizing that?
- ◼ What is the approach?
- ◼ What size is the advertisement?
- ◼ Is the advertisement appearing in other publications?
- ◼ Are you required to supply artwork for all these variations or will it be adapted by others?
- ◼ Who is booking the advertisement?
- ◼ What is the copy date?
- ◼ What are the production specifications, such as screen recommendation and restrictions.
- ◼ Does the client want to see a visual?
- ◼ Get your client to check your copy before it goes for typesetting
- ◼ Has your client approved the artwork?

LEFT Oval Motor Company.

BELOW Press Ads are inevitably badly printed on poor quality paper, and surrounded by other ads of a similar nature. The successful ad is not the one that wins design awards, but the one which brings in the business for the client.

Many companies who advertise in local papers are small businesses who see the need to advertise but have only limited resources. They are often inexperienced in promotion and may not understand what you require from *them* in order to fulfil their brief. They may not understand how an ad is produced and why you charge for doing the design and artwork. Take the time to explain whatever is necessary.

Deadlines mean that many press ads are designed at artwork stage, but this pressure can inspire good work and is a factor which designers have to learn to cope with.

To produce a prestigious 6-page fold-out brochure that would introduce Tristar Cars to new corporate clients and update existing clients on the company's future plans and expanding services. The brochure was to be full-colour with an attractive glossy finish and designed to fit 2 different formats, the English and American.

The brochure had to communicate three points fundamental to Tristar Cars' success: its use of identical cars internationally through the whole fleet, its efficient booking services and communication using the latest computer technology, and its convenient location in air terminals.

At the very first meeting with the client the key points were discussed and the designer produced a quick thumbnail sketch summarizing his initial ideas and thoughts.

The most important key images were quickly defined as

■ the car and driver to establish the fundamental nature of the business

■ the computer terminal to establish the priority given by Tristar Cars to good communication

■ a map to emphasize the nationwide presence of the company

■ proven evidence of a track record with another major international company

■ the door-to-door service link with major international airlines

The copywriter and designer then worked together to decide on themes in the copy and how they could be expressed in images. One of the major themes was 'spot the difference', there being none – the cars are all the same. The other major theme was the 'we're so good you won't even know we're there'.

ABOVE The main theme of the brochure was to emphasise the quality of service which Tristar Cars offered and this was reflected in the choice of a marbled background.

BELOW LEFT The quick thumbnail produced at speed during the first client meeting formed the basis of the eventual design solution.

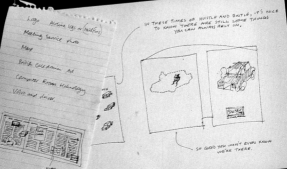

IT'S NICE TO

What would you say if we told you that although we've only got one car," we totalled *14.2 million* passenger miles last year?

What would you say if we told you that every time you book a Tristar Executive Car, the same car arrives?

And what would you say if we told you that we have 150 uniformed drivers to drive one car?

You must be joking!!

Well of course you're right, we are – but not quite in the sense you might think.

You see all our cars are the same – Volvos! Our "one car fleet" actually comprises 150 identical red Volvo 740 Luxury Saloons and Estates – probably the world's safest means of cruising through 14.2 million miles in a year!

That's why each time your Tristar Executive Car arrives, you won't be able to tell it from the last one you hired (unless of course you happen to be a keen number plate spotter!)

And that's why our 150 highly trained drivers

know their vehicles inside out – the surest way know of ensuring a consistently high quality vice, day in day out.

We have chosen Volvos because they are personification of the very highest quality and engineering standards. A unique combination of exceptional driving characteristics and a renowned high of specification, they are all in superbly comfortable, safe reliable vehicle and one we are proud to place at service.

Our hand-picked, highly fessional drivers have all

Fully computerised vehicle control system.

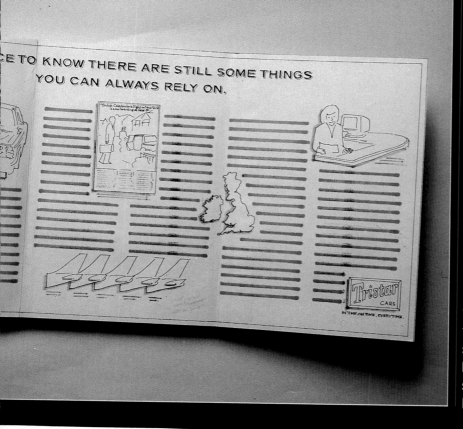

At this point a rough layout worked in magic marker and felt tip on a card (approximating in weight to the final card intended) was presented to the client to show the proposed look and feel of the brochure. A coloured-up rough was deemed unnecessary at this stage at the layout was the critical consideration.

Once the key images had been defined, the copywriter was tightly briefed to write to an accurate word count. The copy was written and fitted by a combination of adjusting primarily the sizes but also the positions of the images.

The positions of the images on the rough layout were altered slightly by the client before the final layout to reflect better their relative importance to potential customers.

The marbled background was chosen to give a feeling of quality of finish and the typeface selected, Walbaum, with its clean Bodoni-style fine serif face to echo the elegance of the marble. The headlines were set in Venus, a contrasting modern sans serif outlined face. The type was heavily leaded to give air and legibility.

TOP LEFT The visual presented to the client was a simple black and white outline. The main headline was rendered in because it helped present the idea, but other text was simply indicated by marker lines.

LEFT Although the emphasis of some of the final images was amended slightly by the client, the end result changed very little from the original visual.

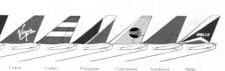

sleeve for the single 'So Good Now' released on Chrysalis records. This single was recorded live on an American tour and the client wanted this made clear. Size and stock to be standard.

The music industry is highly competitive with record companies all vying for rack space in stores, particularly in the busy pre-Christmas period. Record sleeve design is regarded as being one of the fastest moving areas of graphic design, and depending on the urgency of a release date, a record sleeve can take anything from one hour to several weeks to complete. Most of the records Chrysalis produce are planned several weeks or months in advance of release, but occasionally it is necessary to rush-release a record to order to coincide with an unexpected appearance.

Pop music is a slave to fashion trends, so inevitably many of the products have visual parallels with fast food. Recording artists are also involved in the packaging of their projects. The music industry is full of egos bouncing off walls like squash balls. Designers usually work in close collaboration with recording artists, managers, marketing directors and retail people, and ideas and proposals are discussed thoroughly at the briefing stage. The company policy for design is to resolve as many of the creative problems as possible at the 'rough' stage.

Good design and packaging generates interest in a product and persuades the potential customer into parting with money. This first rule of marketing is especially true in the entertainments industry where competition is fierce and the market very transient.

Record distribution houses cannot stockpile vast quantities of paper and plastic, so often a record and cover will be manufactured at the last minute, depending on a chart position and retail orders. An hour spent on corrections can affect an important delivery by anything up to a week. Deadlines and delivery dates are established with print production as soon as roughs are approved.

Expertise in all areas of print and mass-production – particularly lithography and silkscreen – is imperative for a designer working in the record

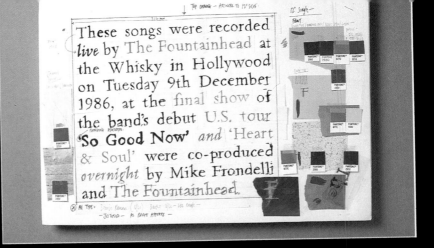

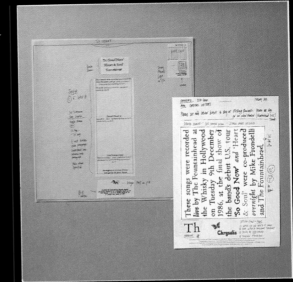

ABOVE AND RIGHT The original roughs were prepared very quickly, together with colour ways and a type mark-up.

LEFT Letterspacing in the type was essential. Letterspacing cannot always be done so well by the typesetter.

industry. Most covers are produced by lithography, using the four process colours or the Pantone matching system. A single, or album, cover involves logotype design, cover, posters, press advertising and occasionally supervision of related merchandising. The Fountainhead *So Good Now* sleeve was commissioned from me at 11 o'clock one morning, the roughs were prepared over lunch, and the paste-up completed by our outside suppliers the following morning.

The group involved were working in Ireland on a tour, and were unable to be in London for a meeting, and so my ideas were proposed over the telephone and roughed out on tracing paper with their manager standing over me. I tactfully rejected a rather predictable photograph, and finalized the layout which included a block of justified Bembo type with all the relevant information in different colours. I always keep ideas for colours in a notebook. I also suggested using bright, solid Pantone colours and silver on an industrial textured card. The sleeve was eventually printed on the reverse side of our standard white sided board, using the imperfection in the rough stock.

LEFT Try keeping ideas for colours in a notebook. This ad was part of the promotional material and although the copy is different it retains the changing colour style of the type.

ABOVE Flat proofs of the 7-in (18-cm) sleeve. The reverse side of some standard stock was just as good as the original suggestion for a special textured card.

RIGHT Finished copy of the 12-in (30-cm) sleeve. Most sleeves are laminated, but not this one as lamination would have totally destroyed its tactile quality.

These songs were recorded *live* by The Fountainhead at the Whisky in Hollywood on Tuesday 9th December 1986, at the final show of the band's debut U.S. tour. 'So Good Now', 'Heart & Soul' & 'Sometimes' were co-produced *overnight* by Mike Frondelli and The Fountainhead.

British Airways – wanted a new look for their in-flight magazine, which is distributed free to all passengers. This captive readership, not business travellers but people going on holiday or returning home, would determine the style and content of the magazine and the type of consumer advertising attracted to it. Editorially and visually the product was to be cheerful, with a lively holiday feel to it.

Designs were prepared, based on a selection of new titles suggested. The name of the magazine would have the strongest influence on the visual styling, and so it was a title rather than a design that was finally chosen.

A simple three-column page design was devised and typefaces for text, headings, lead-ins and captions were chosen. To give the editorial pages sufficient identity within the typographical variety of the advertising – this is outside the control of the designer, but constitutes a powerful visual element of the magazine for the reader – it was decided to limit the display type to two styles.

Each issue is planned around the advertising spaces – many of them having previously guaranteed positions. This is done very roughly on miniature flat plans, with no attempt at this stage to design individual pages. Of course copy length, the number and size of illustrations, and the editor's preferences are all considered when making this plan. The degree of pre-layout visualization varies from designer to designer, some preparing quite detailed thumbnails, others going straight ahead from simple roughs. I come between the two.

The page layout and design are then produced in the form of a design paste-up, but not as camera-ready artwork. Galley proofs have to be marked up to indicate headings and the positions of illustrations, to act as a guide for the printer and for the approval of editor and client.

This paste-up goes both to the typesetter as the instruction for complete page make-up, and to the reproduction house, which scans the originals and supplies colour proofs for all the illustrations. Their work is married together to produce an ozalid proof. The ozalid and the colour proofs are amended and corrected as required before printing.

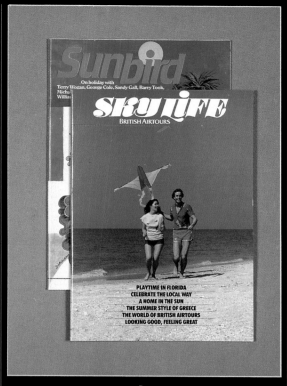

LEFT The original cover visuals were as much an exercise in deciding a title for the magazine as creating the graphic style. The name itself would dictate the style.

ABOVE It was eventually decided to call the magazine 'Skylife' which instantly suggested a more sophisticated style than 'Sunbird', the original name.

RIGHT 3 spreads from the first issue. Magazines develop and change gradually over time, but the basic style should show through. In-flight magazines have a captive audience – in this case holiday makers – so the content and style are lively and cheerful.

VIDEO FOR 'BARCLAYS HOME MORTGAGE'

███████ **This video was to be shown in banks to advertise Barclays Home Mortgage scheme. One of the main marketing features was that the mortgage was available for any type of domestic property. Although the video would have a music track, the sound would be turned down for most of the time, so the video had to be designed as a silent sequence.** Captions would provide the information normally conveyed by a voice-over narration, but I was determined to keep the typography to a minimum and communicate the idea through the animation.

I knew that the style of the video would be tied up with the treatment of the buildings. I had already considered showing the process of finding and buying a house using a game format, but while researching board games I came across sets of building bricks and decided to use the bricks — a rather obvious, but apt, unifying theme. Bricks also gave me a way of building other necessary objects, such as bar charts, and a title logo using the same elements.

The construction-kit treatment was also an ideal candidate for computer animation, which was the only means of achieving the polished level of production required within a seven-week schedule. It would be costly, but after the initial design the logistics would be straightforward.

The computer system to be used was the Bosch F.G.S. 4000, at the Moving Picture Company, which would give extremely good value for the budget we had. The only drawback of this system was its inability to give the visual feedback of real-time animation while planning the animation.

Scrambling to keep ahead of the schedule, I tackled the more basic elements, such as the brick alphabet and the simpler objects, to keep a flow of work going through the computer department. Then I concentrated on the more elaborate details of the buildings. One of these designs, an ornate Victorian gothic mansion, caused problems. It became obvious when I handed over this drawing that it was going to soak up a disproportionate amount of the computer schedule, so after a bit of horse-trading with the computer team I modified the number of elements in it.

In two scenes I'd incorporated Mr and Mrs

Average, a couple of doll-like figures, the kind often sold with children's construction kits. Although their design was very basic, they were more sculptural than the bricks and couldn't easily be digitized directly from drawings, so I commissioned a 2ft-high polystyrene model of each figure. These were then covered with a network of polygons and the various points measured with a 3-D digitizer.

I was shown first-draft animations of the scenes and although many of these were subsequently modified, some of the more elaborate ones worked perfectly at this stage. Editing the rough assembly of the whole video, a mixture of completed scenes and line tests was an important stage in the schedule. It served two purposes. It was an indication to the client of work in progress and it was a guide for a composer to start work on the music track.

At the final video edit, the completed scenes were assembled and the typographic captions were superimposed by means of a character generator.

It's rare that I stick rigidly to the original storyboard, frame by frame. I always find that there's room to develop and refine the basic ideas, as long as they remain true to the original concept in the client's eyes and don't generate extra cost or time. On the whole, the changes I made sharpened up the original ideas considerably, but towards the end of the schedule I experienced, as I often do, the nagging feeling that I would like to have tackled the project differently. I regretted not having made a set of jumbo toy bricks, which I could have arranged to form the various structures, instead of working on drawings of the houses and the other elements. This would have been truer to the basic concept.

RIGHT Building bricks became the main theme for the video and they were used to build images. The visual effect of the video was important because although there was a soundtrack, the pictures had to stand on their own as a silent sequence.

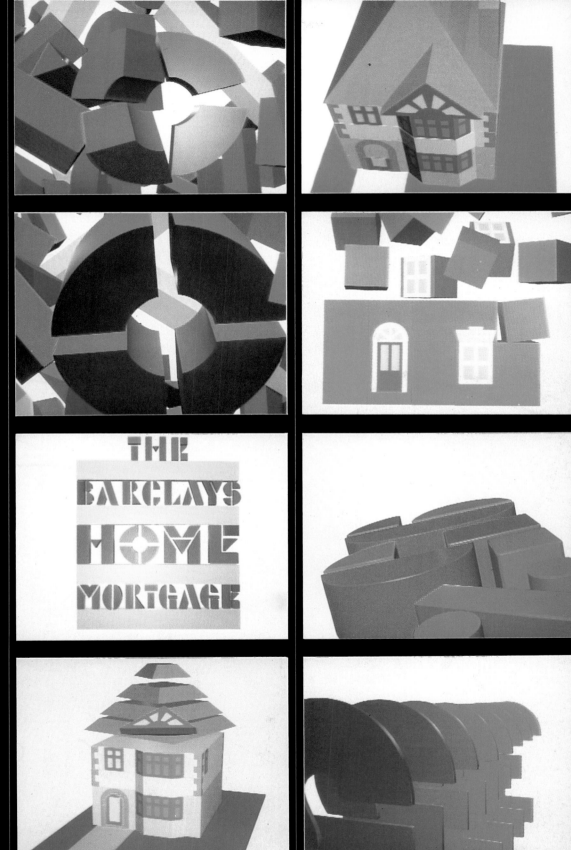

specializing in literature, packaging, and company identity design. The design of Alto's own image was, therefore, extremely important, enabling them to demonstrate their creative abilities in this area. The brief called for a striking contemporary image that was used with style and flair.

Work began on designing the basic elements of the identity. The design team considered the problem from several different aspects. Should the image or logo be based on the name 'Alto', or on the initial letters 'ADG'? Would a symbol be more appropriate? It was finally agreed that the logo should be based on a capital 'A', used along with 'ALTO' in a contrasting formal serif typeface.

The main use of the new identity was to be for the company's stationery. Designs were produced for a letterhead, compliments slip and visiting card. The image was thought to work well with the 'A' logo printed in strong colours, and 'ALTO' blind embossed, running vertically along the righthand edge of the paper. The typeface used was Largo Light, which has only a capital alphabet. The designer created a house style, combining large initial letters with smaller capitals, and, in conjunction with the typesetter, produced a master guide, illustrating usage in a variety of type sizes. The information – name, address, directors – and the company logo were positioned on the letterhead to leave the greatest area of the paper for typing. An alignment guide for the typist was provided by the lefthand edge of the typography at the top and bottom of the heading. Fold and centre guides were also printed on the A4 sheet.

The final dummy was produced to closely resemble the printed heading. The type and 'A' logo were produced using dry transfer coloured letters, and the blind embossed 'ALTO' was imitated by cutting the letters from an identical style and weight of paper, and mounting them in position on the layout. This replica of the printed letterhead enabled the final decision to be made, and the design was adopted as the new company identity.

Finished artwork was produced for all the stationery items. In those instances when embos-

ABOVE The anonymous impact of this matt black tube was a considered stage in publicizing the new corporate identity.

RIGHT AND BELOW Each poster was accompanied by a certificate of authenticity to enhance its perceived value to the individual.

ACHIEVING
NEW
HEIGHTS
IN
DESIGN
FOR
MARKETING

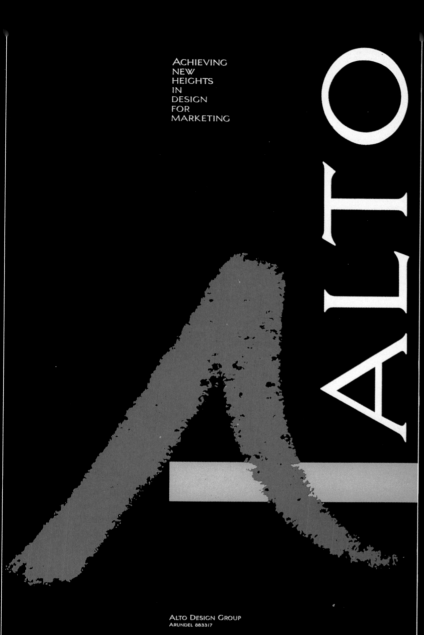

ALTO DESIGN GROUP
ARUNDEL 883317

ABOVE The main use of the new identity was for company stationery. The impact of the stationery was a measure of its success.

BELOW The style was extended onto address and artwork labels.

ABOVE The finished Alto poster 16½ x 23½ in (42 x 60 cm).

sing could not be used, because of practicality and cost, the word 'ALTO' was printed in the same shade of grey used for the rest of the typography.

A limited-edition poster was produced to publicize the new identity. The company logo and namestyle were the main elements used on the poster, which was silkscreen printed using a matt black ink for the background with a combination of glossy orange and blue for the logo. The poster, together with an explanatory leaflet that was numbered and embossed with the company seal, was distributed by post in a matt black tube with an anonymous address label.

CHAPTER SIX

GLOSSARY

ABSORBENT PAPER Unsized paper with the ability to take up moisture or liquid.

ACCOUNT DIRECTOR Senior person dealing with a client, in charge of handling high-level contact with the client's management.

ACETATE A transparent cellulose sheet available in matt or gloss, and in varying thicknesses. It can be used for any type of overlay or as a surface in animation, where individual sheets are used to record every small change in a sequence of movement.

ACKNOWLEDGEMENT Any statement expressing thanks for contributions to a work from organizations or individuals.

ACRYLIC A polymer based on synthetic resin. Most paints with an acrylic emulsion base can be mixed and diluted with water. They dry to a tough, flexible, waterproof finish.

'ADAPT'/ADAPTATION An advertisement modified to a different format.

ADVANCE money paid to an author or other contributor in advance of publication, chargeable against subsequent royalty payments.

ADVERTISER The person or company on whose behalf an advertisement is placed.

AGAINST THE GRAIN Folding or marking paper at right-angles to the grain.

AGATE A size of type about 51–52 point.

AIR (US) A large amount of white space in layout.

AIRBRUSH, AIRBRUSHING A mechanical painting tool producing a fine spray of paint or ink, used in illustration, design and photographic retouching.

ALIGN To square up type or any other graphic components to a horizontal or vertical line.

ALPHABET/ALPHABET LENGTH A measure derived from the length in points of the 26 alphabet letters set in lower case. Thus 39 characters have a measure of 1½ alphabets.

ANIMATIC Simple cut-out animation used to demonstrate an idea for a television advertisement to a client.

ANIMATION A method of film-making that produces movement by rapid projection of a series of sequential still images, usually drawings or cartoons.

ANNOTATION (1) A type label added to an illustration. (2) Explanatory notes.

ANTIQUE PAPER Paper with a rough, lightly sized finish used mainly for books, booklets and folders.

APERTURE The opening behind a camera lens that allows light to penetrate to the film. The size of the aperture is variable, governed by the diaphragm and measured by the f number.

APPENDIX Matter subordinate to the text of a work and printed after it. An appendix may enlarge on information in the text or substantiate it by means of graphs, statistics etc.

ARABIC NUMERALS The numerical symbols 1 2 3 4 5 6 7 8 9 0.

ART BUYER Staff member who commissions specialist photography, illustration and artwork.

ART DIRECTOR Member of the creative team responsible for visualizing the original creative concepts.

ART PAPER Paper with a hard, smooth surface given by an even coating of

ART STUDIO Team of graphic personnel who complete a more finished style for client presentation and finished artwork.

ARTWORK Matter other than text prepared for reproduction, such as illustrations, diagrams and photographs.

ASCENDER The section of a lower case letter rising above the x-height, eg the upper part of an h or d.

ASA (ADVERTISING STANDARDS AUTHORITY)
(1) The organization which handles public complaints about advertising (other than TV and radio) and is also responsible for administering the application of the British Code of Advertising Practice. (2) American Standards Association. An ASA number appears on film stock packaging to provide a basic quantity from which the length and f number of exposure can be calculated.

AUTHOR'S ALTERATION/CORRECTION (US/UK) Changes in copy made by the author after typesetting, but not those made necessary by printer's errors.

AUTHOR'S PROOFS Galley proofs checked and marked by the printer's reader to be read by the author, who may then make any corrections.

AUTOLITHOGRAPHY Printing from an image hand-drawn directly onto a lithographic stone or plate.

AUTOTYPE A process that converts a PMT (stat) of original lettering into dry transfer form, in any specified colour.

AVA/AUDIO VISUAL AIDS Teaching and display equipment such as projectors, video recorders etc.

BACK TO BACK (US) Printing on both sides of a sheet of paper.

BACK UP To print the second side of a sheet of paper. Backed refers to the sheet when it has been backed-up.

BACKGROUND The area over which the main images or components are superimposed.

BANK PAPER A light, uncoated paper used for making carbon copies.

BANNER A main headline across the full width of the page.

BAR CODE A pattern of lines identifying details of a product, such as country of origin, manufacture and type of product, conforming to the universal product code. The pattern is read by a computer-controlled sensor for stock control purposes.

BARYTA PAPER Paper coated with barium sulphate gelatin used for text impressions on typesetting machines.

BASE ARTWORK Artwork requiring the addition of other elements eg halftone positives, before reproduction.

BASE LINE (1) An imaginary line on which the bases of capitals rest. (2) (US) The last line of space on a page containing text matter.

BELOW-THE-LINE Advertising term describing costs of promotional items other than the advertisement itself.

BILLBOARD A large-scale outdoor method of advertising ranging from posters to sophisticated, electronic moving images.

BINDING The securing of the printed pages and outer cover of a publication transforming it into a book, magazine, brochure etc.

BLACK LETTER Old style of typeface based on broad-nib script, also called Gothic (UK) and Old English (US).

BLAD Sample pages of a book produced in booklet form for promotional purposes.

BLEED (1) An image that extends to the edge of the paper or page without leaving any free space. (2) When ink or paint is applied to an unsuitable surface and the lines run and blur.

BLIND EMBOSS To make an impression without foil or ink, eg on the case of a book.

BLOCK (1) Halftone or line illustration engraved or etched on a zinc or copper plate, for use in letterpress printing. (2) A metal stamp used to impress a design on a book cover. To block is to emboss a book cover. (3) (US) Metal or wood base on which a plate is mounted to type height.

BLOWUP An enlargement.

BLUELINE (US) Copy made by the whiteprint process in blue lines on a white background.

BLURB The description of a book or author printed on the jacket or on other promotional material.

BODY (1) The shank of a type. (2) The main portion of a book excluding prelims or appendices.

BODY COPY/MATTER/TYPE (1) Printed matter forming the main part of a work, but not including headings etc. (2) (US) Body type refers to the actual type used in setting a text.

BODY SIZE Point measurement of a body of type as cast.

BOLD, BOLD FACE Type with a conspicuously heavy black appearance. It is based on the same design as a medium weight type in the same fount.

BOND PAPER Standard grade of evenly finished paper used for writing, typing and printing.

BOOK JACKET The printed paper cover folded around the case in which a book is sold.

BOOK MAKEUP (US) The collation and identification of copy prepared for printing.

BOX, BOX RULE An item of type or other graphic matter ruled off on all four sides with a heavy rule or border.

BRASS A bookbinder's engraved plate used to block a book cover.

BRIEF The initial instructions for a project given to the artist, either directly from a client or agency.

BRISTOL BOARD Fine board made in various thicknesses and qualities, usually of smooth finish, used for drawing and printing.

BROADSIDE/BROADSHEET Old term for a sheet of paper printed on one side.

BROCHURE A pamphlet or other unbound, short publication.

BROMIDE (1) A photographic print on bromide paper. (2) A proof from photocomposition, made on paper rather than on film.

BULK (1) The thickness of the assembled pages of a book. (2) The thickness of a sheet of paper relating to its weight.

BURNISH The rubbing down of dry transfer forms.

C

C-TYPE A method, developed by Kodak, of processing colour prints directly from a negative.

CALLIGRAPHY Derived from the Greek words kallos (beauty) and graphein (to write), calligraphy is the art of producing fine writing.

CAMERA-READY Term applied to artwork that is ready to be photographed for reproduction.

CAPITAL, CAP The term for upper case letters deriving from the style of inscription at the head, or capital, of a Roman column.

CAPS AND SMALLS Type consisting of capitals for initials and small caps in place of lower case letters.

CAPTION Strictly speaking the descriptive matter printed as a headline above an illustration, but also generally used to refer to information printed underneath or beside a picture.

CAPTION BOARD Artwork for film titles or studio use when making videotape titles.

CARBON PAPER A thin sheet of paper coated on one side with carbon. When the coated side is placed over a sheet of paper and another sheet is placed on top, an image drawn, typed or written onto the top sheet will be duplicated through the carbon onto the underlying sheet.

CARD RATES Quoted rates for advertising. The negotiated cost of a commercial spot may be subject to one or more discounts.

CARICATURE A drawing of a person or thing showing deliberate distortion with comic or satirical intent.

CARTRIDGE PAPER A good all-round paper with a rough surface, particularly suitable for drawing and offset printing.

CASE (1) The stiff cover of a book, consisting of two boards, a hollow and a binding material. (2) A box with separate compartments in which pieces of type are kept. This is the origin of the term lower case and upper case.

CASTING OFF Making a calculation as to how much space manuscript copy will take up when printed in a given typeface.

CATCHLINE Word put at the top of a page or over a piece of type to indicate its place in the whole.

CENTRED Type which is placed centrally on a sheet or type measure.

CHAPTER DROP The level at which text begins underneath a chapter heading.

CHARACTER (1) An individual item cast in type, eg a letter, figure, punctuation mark, sign or space. (2) A set of symbols in data processing which represents a figure, letter etc.

CHARACTER COUNT The number of characters (1) in a piece of copy, or in a line or paragraph.

CHROMOLIN A fast proofing system in which powders are used instead of inks.

CIBACHROME Agfa process, a direct method of obtaining photographic colour prints.

CIRCULAR ADVERTISING Matter in the form of a single leaf or folded sheet.

CLASSIFIED AD Newspaper or magazine advertisement without illustrations, sold by the line.

CLEAN PROOF A printer's proof that is free of errors.

COATED PAPER Paper that has had a mineral coating applied to the surface to improve the finish.

COCKED UP INITIAL (RAISED CAPITAL) A bold face capital that projects above the line of type.

COCKLE The wrinkle or pucker in paper.

COLLAGE The art of using cut-out shapes to create an image, sometimes utilizing mixed media.

COLLATE To put the sections or pages of a book in correct order.

COLOPHON (1) An emblem identifying a printer or publisher appearing usually on the spine and title page of a book. (2) An inscription usually placed at the end of a book giving the title, printer's name and location and date of printing.

COLOUR BAR A set of standardized bars carried on all colour proofs in the four-colour process, enabling the printer to check at a glance the density of the colour and the amount of ink used.

COLOUR CHART Chart used in colour printing to standardize and select or match coloured inks and tints.

COLOUR CORRECTION The adjustment of colour values in reproduction to obtain a correct image.

COLOUR PROOFS Printed sheets that are run off to enable the artist, client and printer to check colour accuracy and register prior to final printing.

COLOUR SEPARATION Division of colours in a continuous tone, multicoloured original or line copy into basic portions by a process of photographic filtration. The portions are reproduced by a separate printing plate carrying a colour.

COLOUR SEPARATIONS The number of images or pieces (subjects) to be separated in the colour separation

COLOUR TRANSPARENCY A positive photographic image produced in colour on transparent film.

COMB BINDING Mechanical binding method in which slots are driven through the cover and pages, then secured with plastic fingers.

COMMAND An instruction given to a computer by its operator.

COMMERCIAL Any advertising on TV or radio, as opposed to print media.

COMMERCIAL ART A term used to describe artwork intended for use in advertising or promotion, as distinct from fine art.

COMMERCIAL ARTIST A person undertaking finished artwork.

COMMISSION A 15% deduction from quoted rates allowed to recognized advertising agencies by certain television channels. The advertiser may negotiate partial repayment of commission or pay additional fees to the agency.

COMPASS Instrument used for drawing circles and arcs. It consists of two legs connected by an adjustable joint, one carrying a metal point and the other a lead.

COMPOSE To set copy in type.

COMPOSING ROOM The area of a printing works specifically designated for typesetting and makeup.

COMPOSITE ARTWORK Artwork combining a number of different elements.

COMPOSITOR The person responsible for setting type, whether by hand or machine.

COMPUTER GRAPHICS The use of computers to generate an output of information in graphic form as in a picture, diagram or printed characters.

CONCERTINA FOLD/FANFOLD Method of paper folding in which each fold runs in the opposite direction to the one before to form a pleated effect.

CONDENSED A typeface with an elongated narrow appearance.

CONSUMER Buyer, potential buyer or non-buyer of product, brand or service.

CONSUMER RESEARCH Research into the numbers, characteristics, preferences and behaviour of consumers.

CONTACT PRINT, CONTACTS Photographic print or prints made by direct contact with an original positive or negative at same size.

CONTACT SCREEN A halftone screen made on a film base which has a graded dot pattern. It is used in direct contact with a film or plate to obtain a halftone negative from a continuous tone original. It provides better definition than the conventional glass screen.

CONTENTS A page of a book listing the articles or chapters in it.

CONTINUOUS TONE Photographs or coloured originals in which the subjects contain continuous shades between the lightest and the darkest tones, without being broken up by dots.

CONTRAST The distinction range between tones in a photograph in the range from black to white.

COPY Matter to be set in type.

COPY-DATE The date by which copy must be submitted.

COPYWRITING The writing of copy specifically for use in advertising.

CORPORATE IDENTITY/HOUSESTYLE The elements of design by which a company or other institution establishes a consistent and recognizable identity through communication, promotion and distribution material.

COVER-PAPERS Papers for the covers of books, artwork, pamphlets etc.

COVERAGE Also known as net coverage or reach. The number of people in a particular target group who have the opportunity to see or hear an advertisement at least once. It is expressed as a percentage, or sometimes in thousands.

CROP, CROPMARK The part of a photograph or illustration that is discarded after it has been trimmed.

CROPPING AID Two L-shaped pieces of cardboard which can be moved over an image until the most complimentary position for cropping is found.

CROSS-HEAD Subsection, paragraph heading or numeral printed in the body of text, usually marking the first subdivision of a chapter.

CROWN Standard size of printing paper 15 × 20 in (381 × 508 mm).

CROWNER The lid of a point-of-sale display that folds back to make a show card.

CURSOR A moving symbol on a VDU used as a reference point by the operator for arranging on the screen.

CUT-OUT An image that is cut out from its original background, leaving an outline shape.

CYAN A shade of blue used in four-colour printing

D

DAISY WHEEL PRINTER A typewriter mechanism common to word processor systems with a flat circular head for printing characters.

DASHES Punctuation marks used to denote a pause in a sentence before expanding on a previous statement.

DATA PROCESSING The processing of information via a computer or other mechanical or electronic device.

DATABASE A general computer file of information that can be drawn upon or updated by all users having access, but without imposing a limited or specific use of the file.

DESCENDER The part of a lower case letter that falls below the x-height.

DETAIL PAPER/LAYOUT PAPER A thin, translucent paper with a hard surface used for layouts and sketches.

DEVELOPER The chemical used to bring up an image on photographic film, paper, or plate.

DIDOT POINT The continental unit for type. It measures 0.0148 in whereas an English point is 0.013837 in.

DIE An intaglio engraved stamp used for impressing a design.

DIE CUTTING To cut paper, board or card to a particular design with a metal die, for packaging and display

DIE STAMPING A form of printing where all the characters are in relief.

DIGITIZE To convert an image into a form that can be processed, stored and electronically reconstructed.

DRAFT To compose copy or an illustration in a basic form to be refined; or an item so prepared. A final draft is copy that is ready for typesetting.

DROP The number lines of text in a column as allowed on the grid.

DROP CAP A large initial at the beginning of a text that drops into the lines of type below.

DROP FOLIOS The numbers printed at the bottom of each page.

DROP SHADOW A shadow behind an image designed to bring the image forward.

DRY MOUNTING The use of heat-sensitive adhesives.

DRY TRANSFER LETTERING Characters transferred to the page by being rubbed off the back of a sheet.

DRY TRANSFER SHEETS Sheets holding letters, images, tones etc, that can be transferred onto a surface by applying pressure to the reverse side of the sheet.

DUMMY The prototype of a proposed book in the correct format, paper and bulk but with blank pages.

DUOTONE Also called a duplex halftone, an illustration process using two colours. Two negatives are made from a monochrome original, one for the darker shade with the greater detail, often black, the other for the lighter colour.

DUPE Duplicate.

DYE TRANSFER PRINT A method of making photographic colour prints using gelatin relief matrices. A matrix is made for each of the three primary colours, red, yellow and blue and soaked in appropriate dye solution. These are then placed in turn on a gelatin-coated paper that absorbs dye from each to produce the full image.

E

EDITING To prepare a manuscript for publication.

EDITION The whole number of copies of a work printed and issued at one time.

EGYPTIAN A group of display types with heavy slab serifs and little contrast in the thickness of strokes.

ELLIPSE A regular oval shape that corresponds to an oblique view of a circular plane.

EM A unit of linear measurement, 12 points or 4.5mm.

EM QUAD A space in type that is the square of the type size.

EM RULE/DASH used in punctuating text, the length of one em.

EMBOSSING Relief printing or stamping in which dies are used to raise letters above the surface of paper, cloth or leather.

EMULSION The light sensitive coating of a photographic material.

EMULSION DOWN In making a printing plate, the direct contact of film with emulsion side down on a plate. If the emulsion is uppermost the image formed is slightly haloed due to the thickness of the film.

EN A measurement half the width of an em, used in casting off.

EN QUAD A space in type half the width of an em quad.

EN RULE/DASH A dash (–), approximately half an em.

END PAPERS The leaves of paper at the front and back of a book which cover the inner sides of the boards, securing the book to its case.

ENGRAVER The person responsible for making the colour-separated films from which the printing plates derive, even if this is done electronically.

ENGRAVING The design or lettering etched on a plate or block and also the print taken from such a plate.

ETCHING Designing on a metal plate treated with acid to eat out the lines, and with other areas protected by the application of a ground. It is also a print taken from the etched plate.

EXPOSURE The amount of light allowed to contact a photosensitive material. The exposure is the combination of length of contact and intensity of light acting upon the material.

F

FACE The printing surface of any type character. It also refers to the group or family to which any particular type design belongs, as in typeface.

FASHION BOARDS Simple body boards lined with good rag paper on one side, and thin paper on the other to prevent warping.

FAT FACE A typeface with extreme contrast in the widths of thin and thick strokes.

FAX, FACSIMILE A slang term applied particularly to an image reproduced by electronic scanning techniques.

FEET The base of a piece of type. It is recessed at the centre to form two 'feet' on which it stands.

FELT SIDE The top side or printing side of paper.

FILLER An extra figure or piece of copy in a magazine or newspaper added to fill space in a page or column.

FILLING IN/UP A fault in printing when ink fills spaces between halftone dots or the counters of type to produce small areas of solid tone.

FILM (1) Transparent plastic material, usually cellulose acetate. (2) Cellulose acetate coated with light-sensitive emulsion for photographic recording of an image.

FILM NEGATIVE A photographic image on film in which the highlights and shadows are reversed; also used extensively in reprographic printing.

FILM POSITIVE (1) A black image on a background of clear or translucent film. (2) A positive image on a film base made as a contact print from stripped negatives. It is used as a mask in intaglio platemaking.

FILTER A gelatin, glass or plastic sheet which may be placed over or in front of a camera lens to alter the colour or quality of light passed through to the film.

FINAL DRAFT Copy fully prepared for typesetting.

FINE RULE A line of hairline thickness.

FISH EYE LENS A wide angle lens that produces a distorted image with a pronounced apparent curve.

FIXED WORD SPACING A method of typesetting employing a standard size for spaces between words, leaving lines unjustified.

FLAT COLOUR Solid areas of colour without any tone.

FLAT PLAN (1) A diagrammatic plan of the pages of a book used to establish the distribution of colour, chapter lengths etc. (2) A diagram or chart showing the sequence of events involved in a process or activity.

FLIPPY, FLIPPY FLOPPY A floppy disc usable on both sides.

FLOP A photomechanical image that has been deliberately or accidentally reversed left to right.

FLOPPY DISC Magnetic disc made of flexible plastic.

FLOWCHART (1) A schematic diagram showing the sequence of a process or related series of events. (2) The plan of a book shown as a sequential drawing of the proposed design and layout of pages.

FOCAL POINT An area on which the eye is forced to focus.

FOIL An extremely thin, flexible metal sheet applied as decoration to a blocked or embossed design.

FOLDED AND GATHERED SHEETS/F & GS Copy which is collated but not trimmed and sent to the publisher for approval of printing before binding begins.

FOLDOUT An extension to the leaf of a book, making it wider than the standard page width which is folded back onto the page.

FOLIO (1) The book size formed when a sheet is folded making the pages half the size of the sheet. (2) A leaf of paper numbered only on the front. (3) A page number and the running headline of a page.

FOOLSCAP Standard size of printing paper 13½ × 17 in (343 × 432 mm).

FORMAT The general appearance or style of a book.

FORMATTING To program standard commands for a computer used in photocomposition, corresponding to directions in the type mark-up.

FORME, FORM Type matter and blocks assembled into pages and locked up in a chase ready for letterpress printing.

FORTY-EIGHT-SHEET A standard poster size measuring 120 × 480 in (305 × 1220 cm).

FOUNT A complete supply of a typeface.

FOUR-COLOUR PROCESS A method of printing in full colour by colour separation, producing four plates for printing in cyan, yellow, magenta and black.

FREEHAND A way of working without artificial aids. Can be applied to drawing, airbrushing etc.

FREEPOST Postage-paid address or envelope for use at no cost to the sender.

FRENCH CURVES A set of clear plastic line-guides designed to provide as many different degrees of curve as possible.

FRONTISPIECE An illustration facing the title page of a book.

FULL MEASURE The width of a line of type as measured in picas.

FULL OUT An instruction to the printer to set type with lines starting at the margin, that is not indented.

FULL POINT A full stop.

G

GAGS Short lines of copy, usually provided by an agency to accompany the illustrations in a storyboard. They are chiefly designed to give the client an even clearer idea of the proposed sequence of events for a filmed advertisement.

GSM, GRAMS PER SQUARE METRE A unit of measurement of paper weight used in printing.

GALLEY Long, shallow, metal tray used by compositors to hold type after it has been set.

GALLEY PROOF Proofs taken from the galley before copy is divided into pages.

GATEFOLD A paper fold in which both sides are folded across the middle of the sheet in overlapping layers.

GLOSSARY A list giving definitions of terms related to a particular subject.

GOLD BLOCKING The stamping of a design on a book cover using gold leaf and a heated die or block.

GOLDEN SECTION The division of a line to give harmonious proportions. If a line is divided unequally the relationship of the two sections should be the same as that of the larger section to the whole. It is in practice a ratio of about 8:13.

GOLFBALL A colloquial term for the printing head of a typewriter in the form of a faceted ball, originally a feature of IBM machines.

GOUACHE Opaque watercolour for which the pigments are mixed with white lead, bone ash or chalk.

GRADATION The smooth transition from one tone or colour to another, or the range of values between black and white.

GRAIN (1) The pattern of fibres in a manufactured sheet. (2) The density of tiny silver crystals in a photographic emulsion.

GRANT PROJECTOR (UK) Electrically-powered piece of equipment for scaling an image up or down. The image is placed onto a lit copyboard below a lens and glass viewing screen. The sized image is projected through the lens up onto the screen where it can then be traced.

GRAPHIC DESIGN Design based on or involving two-dimensional processes, eg illustration, typography, photography, and printing methods.

GRAPHICS TABLET A device for plotting coordinates used in giving information to a computer, using a flat board and an electromagnetic pen.

GRAVURE An intaglio printing process.

GRID A measuring guide used by designers to help ensure consistency.

GRIPPER EDGE The edge which is caught by the grippers as a sheet of paper is fed into a cylinder press.

GRIPPERS On job presses, these are the iron fingers attached to the platen to keep the sheet in place and take it off the type after the impression. On cylinder presses, they are the short curved metal fingers attached to an operating rod which grip the sheet and carry it round the impression.

GROUND A thin coating made from pitch, gummastic, asphaltum and beeswax which protects the non-image-bearing parts of an etching plate from the action of the acid.

GUILLOTINE A machine for cutting a large number of sheets of paper accurately.

GUTTER A term used in imposition for the space made up of foredges of pages plus the trim. Commonly, the channel down the centre of a page is incorrectly described as the gutter.

H

HAIRLINE RULE The thinnest rule that is possible to print.

HAIRLINES The very fine strokes of a typeface.

HAIRSPACE Mainly used for letter spacing, the very narrow space between type.

HALF-TITLE The title of a book as printed on a leaf preceding the title page.

HALF UP Artwork completed 50% larger than its printed size.

HALFTONE A continuous tone image which is broken down into a series of dots by a cross-line screen. The gradated tones are achieved by variations in the size and density of the dots.

HALFTONE Process by which continuous tone is simulated by a pattern of dots of varying size. A halftone block is a zinc or copper printing plate prepared by this process.

HALFTONE SCREEN A sheet of glass or film bearing a network of lines ruled at right-angles. The screen is used to translate the subject of a halftone illustration into dots.

HARD COPY (1) A copy on paper of matter prepared for printing, used for revision or checking. (2) A computer printout for checking input to the machine.

HARDBACK BOOK/HARDCOVER BOOK (UK/US) A cased book with a stiff board cover.

HARD EDGE The outline of an image that is sharp and well defined.

HEADLINE The title of a book as printed at the top of every page of text.

HICKIE, HICKEY A spot with a blank halo which occurs in printing due to a speck of dust or hard substance adhering to the printing plate or blanket.

HIGHLIGHT The lightest tones of a photograph or illustration.

HOLOGRAM/HOLOGRAPH (1) An image with three-dimensional illusionism created by the action of lasers. (2) In publishing, the term holograph refers to a manuscript hand-written by the author.

HOT METAL General term for composing machines casting single pieces of type from molten metal.

HOUSE STYLE (1) The style of spelling, punctuation and spacing used in a printing or publishing house to ensure consistent treatment of copy during typesetting. (2) Corporate identity.

HYPHEN A punctuation mark used in word or line breaks.

I

ILLUSTRATION (1) A drawing, painting, diagram or photograph reproduced in a publication to explain or supplement the text. (2) A term used to distinguish a drawn image from one that is photographed.

IMAGE (1) The visual contents as a whole. (2) An illustration or photograph for reproduction.

IMPERIAL A size of printing and drawing paper 22 × 30 in (56 × 76 mm).

IMPOSE/IMPOSITION To arrange pages of type in a forme so that when the sheet is folded the text will read continuously.

IMPRESSION (1) All copies of a book printed at one time from the same type of plates. (2) The pressure applied to a frame of type by the cylinder or platen.

IN HOUSE A process or service carried out within a company, not bought in from an individual or organization.

INITIAL A large capital often found at the beginning of a chapter. It is usually dropped to a depth of two or three lines below the first line.

INITIAL CAPS Instruction to the printer to set the first letter of a word or phrase as a captial.

INLINE LETTERING Typeface with a white line inside the shape, following the outline of the letter.

INSTANT ART Images or letters created by the use of dry transfer forms.

INTERFACE A jargon word meaning the point of interaction between a machine and its operator or between two technical systems.

INTERNATIONAL PAPER SIZES A range of standard paper sizes adopted by the ISO. The papers are designated A, B and C series and are available in proportionate sizes, divided in ratio to the largest sheet.

INTERNEGATIVE A photographic negative forming the intermediate stage in making a print from a flat original.

ISBN (INTERNATIONAL STANDARD BOOK NUMBER) A reference number given to every published work identifying area of origin, publishers, title and check control, encoded in a 10-digit number. A new ISBN is given to each new edition of a book.

ITALIC Type with a sloping letter. Indicated in a manuscript by a single underline.

IVORY BOARD A smoothly finished white board used for artwork and display printing.

J

JACKET The paper wrapper in which a book is sold.

JINGLE Catchy tune used to accompany a film or radio commercial.

JUSTIFICATION Spacing of words and letters so that each line of text finishes at the same point.

K

KERN, KERNING The part of a letter which overhangs the next.

KEYLINE An outline drawing in artwork that shows the size and position of an illustration or halftone image.

KISS IMPRESSION An impression in which ink is put on paper by the lightest possible surface contact and not impressed into it. This technique is necessary when printing on coated papers.

KNOCKING UP (UK) The adjustment on one or two edges of a pile of sheets so that they can be cut squarely.

LACQUER A clear coating applied to the surface of a printed job to protect against marking and improve appearance.

LAID PAPER Paper showing the wire marks of the mould or dandy roll used in manufacture.

LAMINATE To protect paper or card and give it a glossy surface by applying a transparent plastic coating through heat or pressure.

LANDSCAPE/HORIZONTAL FORMAT (UK/US) An image in which the width is noticeably greater than the height.

LAY DOWN A general term used to describe the placing of material.

LAYOUT A sheet representing how a printed page will look, showing all the components in their correct positions.

LAYOUT PAPER Translucent tough paper used for paste-up or illustration at the rough stage.

LEAD (1) Spaces less than type height which are used to space out headings and text. (2) The main story in a newspaper or the opening story.

LEADED Type which is set with leads between the lines.

LEADER LINE/RULE A line on an image keyed into annotation.

LETRASET Proprietary name for dry transfer lettering on a plastic sheet that is rubbed down on paper or board in preparing artwork, annotation.

LETTERHEAD The heading on a piece of stationery, usually the name, address and telephone number of a business or individual.

LETTERPRESS A printing process. The image is raised and inked to produce an impression. It also refers to the text of a book, including line illustrations but excluding plates.

LETTERSET A term deriving from letterpress and offset, describing a method of offset printing from a relief plate.

LETTERSPACING The insertion of space between the letters of a word to improve the appearance of a line of type.

LIBRARY OF CONGRESS NUMBER A reference number given to the American edition of a book and recorded at the Library of Congress. This is common practice but not required by law.

LIGHT FACE The opposite of bold face.

LIGHT-FAST INK Ink that is not susceptible to fading when exposed to light over a period.

LIGHT TABLE/BOX A table or box with a translucent glass screen surface illuminated from below, used for viewing or working with any photographically produced material, eg transparency stripping, retouching.

LINE AND HALFTONE An illustration process in which line and halftone negatives are combined, printed onto a plate and etched as a unit.

LINE ILLUSTRATION An illustration simply using lines without incorporating any tone.

LINE LOCK A printing plate made of zinc or copper consisting of solid areas and lines. It is reproduced directly from a line drawing without tones. It is mounted on a wooden block to type height.

LINE BOARD A smoothly finished support suitable for line illustrations and artwork.

LINE CONVERSION A photographic process of converting halftone or continuous tone copy into line images. Middle tones are eliminated to increase contrast.

LINE ORIGINAL An original image prepared for line reproduction.

LINEN TESTER A magnifying glass designed for checking the detail of a halftone dot pattern.

LINOCUT A relief printing surface of linoleum on which the background to the design is cut away with a knife, gouge or engraving tool.

LINOTYPE The first keyboard-operated composing machine to employ the principle of the circulating matrix to cast type in solid lines or slugs.

LITH FILM A film used in preparing plates in photochemical reproduction. It omits middle tones and increases contrasts.

LITHOGRAPHY Printing from a dampened, flat surface using greasy ink, based on the principle of the mutual repulsion of oil and water.

LIVE MATTER A forme awaiting printing, stereotyping or electrotyping.

LOGO/LOGOTYPE A word or several letters cast as one unit.

LOOK-/SEE-THROUGH (UK/US) The visibility of an image through paper when seen against the light.

LOOSE LEAF A binding method that allows the easy removal of individual leaves.

LOOSE MASK Any type of mask that does not adhere to the surface.

LOWER CASE The small letters in a fount of type.

MACHINE COMPOSITION Methods of typesetting involving the use of keyboard-operated machines.

MACHINE PROOF A proof taken when corrections marked on the galley proof and page proof have been made. This is the last opportunity for correcting mistakes before printing.

MAGAZINE A storage device such as that which holds the fount in a hot-metal composing machine.

MAGENTA Shade of red ink used in four-colour printing.

MAGIC MARKERS Brand of felt-tip markers.

MAKE-UP (1) The sheet indicating the placing of the various items on a page. (2) The actual assembling of the page.

MAKING READY In printing, the surface on which the paper or plate rests has to be built up in places to give an overall evenness of impression. This is called making ready, and the build-up backing is known as makeready.

MANILLA A tough, buff coloured paper used in the manufacture of stationery.

MANUSCRIPT The written or typed work which an author submits for publication.

MARBLING Decorative paper used for binding books, and sometimes the book edges. It is done by dipping the sheet in a bath of colours floating on a surface of gum. The colours do not mix but can be combined into patterns with the use of a comb, and transfer readily to the paper surface.

MARGINS The blank areas on a printed page which surround the printed matter.

MARKED PROOF The galleys, supplied to the author for correction. It contains the corrections and queries made by the printer's reader.

MARK UP To mark up is to specify every detail needed for the compositor to set the copy. The mark-up is copy with instructions written on it.

MARKERS Coloured felt – or fibre-tipped pens.

MASK (1) A material used to block out part of an image in photography, illustration or layout. (2) A photographc image modified in tone or colour.

MASKING FILM A transparent film with a low-tack adhesive backing widely used in airbrushing. The mask can be cut in position on the surface, allowing greater accuracy.

MASKING TAPE Tape coated with a low-tack adhesive. It can be used as a mask and is ideal for attaching transparencies to layouts because it can be peeled off.

MASTHEAD Details about a publisher printed on the editorial or contents page of a newspaper or periodical.

MATRIX (1) The brass dies used in hot-metal composition. (2) The impression in papier-mâché taken from a page of type for stereotyping after moulding.

MEASURE The width of a line of text usually measured in pica ems.

MECHANICAL (US) A term for camera-ready copy or artwork.

MECHANICAL TINTS Tints consisting of dot or line patterns that can be laid down on artwork before or during reproduction processing.

MEDIA Plural term used in referring to information sources, eg radio, television, publishing etc.

MEDIA BUYER Executive responsible for buying advertising space.

MEDIA PLANNER Person in charge of advertising and/or TV time slots, with the aim of reaching the people most likely to buy a client's products.

MEDIUM Any kind of paint, dye, or colouring agent used to cover a surface.

METALLIC INK A printing ink which produces an effect of gold, silver, copper or bronze.

MEZZOTINT Intaglio printing process producing a range of tones.

MOCK-UP The rough visualization of a publication or packaging design showing size, colour, type etc.

MODERN FACE A typeface with vertical stress, strong stroke contrast and unbracketed fine serifs.

MOIRÉ PATTERN The result of an error in colour separation of a halftone, causing a criss-cross pattern to appear on the illustration.

MONO ADOPTION A single-coloured image taken from a full-colour original.

MONOCHROME An image made up of varying tones but in only one colour.

MONOPHOTO The trade name of the photocomposition system produced by the manufacturers of Monotype.

MONOTYPE (1) The trade name for composing machines which cast single types. (2) The process of making a painting on glass or metal and then taking an impression on paper. Only one impression can be taken.

MONTAGE Assembling portions of several drawings or photographs to form a single original.

MOTTLING An uneven impression, especially in flat areas. It is usually caused by too much pressure or unsuitable paper or ink.

MOUNTING BOARD A heavy board used for mounting photographs or artwork.

MOVEABLE TYPE The principle of an old fashioned method of typesetting in which single pieces of type were used rather than slugs.

MULTIPLE EXPOSURE Variations of the same subject or separate images superimposed to form one image in exposure or processing.

NEGATIVE Photographic film that has been exposed and processed to fix a reverse tone or colour image from which positive prints can be made.

NEWSPRINT The paper used for printing newspapers, characteristically absorbent because it is unsized.

NOT A finish in high quality rag papers, which is midway between rough and hot-pressed.

OCTAVO A sheet of paper folded in half three times, to make eight or sixteen pages. It also refers to a standard broadside divided into eight parts.

OFFPRINT A reprint of an article or other part of a publication, produced as a separate item.

OFFSET LITHOGRAPHY A method of lithography by which the image is not printed direct from the plate but 'offset' first onto a rubber covered cylinder, the blanket, which performs the printing operation.

OLD FACE/OLD STYLE (US) Type form characterized by diagonal stress and sloped, bracketed serifs.

ONE AND A HALF UP Artwork prepared at one and a half times the size at which it will be printed.

OPACITY The term used to describe non-transparency in printing papers.

ORIGAMI Ancient Japanese art of folding paper into intricate shapes.

ORIGINAL Any matter or image intended for reproduction.

ORNAMENT Decorative elements used with type matter, such as flowers, borders etc.

ORPHAN A single word that stands at the top of a page when copy has been set.

OUTLINE LETTERS Typefaces in which the letters are formed with outlines rather than solid strokes.

OVEREXPOSURE A fault in platemaking caused when the light source is too close to the vacuum frame.

OVERHEAD PROJECTOR A machine for projecting images drawn on a transparent acetate slide or roll, by passing the image through an overhead lens and turning it through 90° onto a flat surface.

OVERLAY (1) A transparent sheet used in the preparation of multicolour artwork. (2) A translucent sheet covering a piece of original artwork, on which instructions may be written.

OVERMATTER Matter set which does not fit within the appropriate space.

OVERPRINT Printing over an already printed area.

OVERS, OVERRUNS Paper issued beyond the bare requirements to allow for makeready, spoils etc. It also refers to the quantity produced above the ordered number.

OZALID A trade name referring to a method of copying page proofs by the diazo process.

PACKAGER A company offering a service or commodity as a complete unit or package.

PACKAGING The construction of individual product packs for points-of-sale display.

PAGE MAKE UP (1) In photocomposition, it is a display showing copy as it will appear on a page.

PAGE PROOFS Proofs of type which have been paginated. It refers to the secondary stage in proofing, after galley proofs and before machine proofs.

PAGES TO VIEW The number of pages visible on one side of a sheet that has been printed on both sides.

PAGINATION The term given to numbering the pages of a book.

PAMPHLET A short publication presented unbound and in a soft cover.

PANTONE MATCHING SYSTEM A registered trade name for a system of colour matching in designer's materials such as inks, papers, marker pens.

PARCHMENT Goat or sheepskin, scraped and dressed with lime and pumice and used for writing on.

PARALLEL MOTION A drawing board that holds counterweights and has a straight edge to ensure accurate measurement and positioning.

PASTE-UP A layout of a number of pages used to plan the positioning of illustrations, captions and text.

PERCENTAGE REDUCTION/ENLARGEMENT The method of instructing the sizing of an image for reproduction.

PERFECT BINDING A binding method on which the leaves of a book are trimmed at the back and glued, but not sewn.

PERFORATE (1) Print perforation is to make broken slotted rules so that matter can be torn off. (2) Pin-hole perforation is to punch holes eg in postage stamps.

PERSPECTIVE The art of drawing a three-dimensional object on a flat surface.

PHOTOCOMPOSITION The production of display line and text by photographic means on film or paper. Photocomposing machines assemble lines of letters from various forms of photo matrix.

PHOTOCOPY A copy produced immediately from an original by one of several methods involving photographic techniques.

PHOTOGRAVURE The process of printing from a photomechanically prepared surface, which holds the ink in recessed cells.

PHOTOHEADLINER A machine designed to arrange display type and produce an image by photographic methods.

PHOTOLITHOGRAPHY A method of lithographic printing in which the image is transferred to the plate photographically and printed on a lithographic printing machine.

PHOTOMECHANICAL (1) Methods of making printing plates that involve photographic techniques. (2) The assembly of type or illustrations for transfer to a printing plate.

PHOTOMECHANICAL TRANSFER A mechanical method of quickly producing photoprints from flat originals for use in paste up, presentation visuals etc.

PHOTOMONTAGE The use of images from different photographs combined to produce a new, composite image.

PHOTO-OPAQUE A general term for opaque solutions used to paint out parts of process negatives.

PHOTO-RESTORATION The careful repair of an old or damaged photographic print.

PHOTOSENSITIVE A material treated chemically to become light sensitive.

PHOTOSTAT A facsimile copy of a document – typed, written, printed or drawn.

PICA The old name for 12 points, the unit of measurement used in setting.

PLATE Sheet, usually made of metal, that carries the image for reproduction in the printing process.

PMS Pantone Matching System.

PMT Photomechanical transfer.

POINT Standard unit of type size. In the Anglo-American system it is 0.01388 in, or 72 to the inch. The Continental (Didot) point is calculated differently.

POINT-OF-SALE The term for display equipment and advertising matter placed in a sales area close to the commodity it describes.

POLAROID A trade name of photographic materials capable of self development. The term also covers equipment used with such materials.

PORTRAIT An upright image or page.

POSITIVE (1) An image made photographically on paper or film, usually derived from a negative (2) A photographic colour transparency or film with a positive image, used in platemaking.

POSTER A large-scale display or advertising sign on card or heavy paper.

PRELIMS, PRELIMINARY MATTER The pages preceding the body of a book. They usually consist of half title, title, preface and contents.

PRESENTATION VISUAL Material prepared as a sample of the proposed appearance of a printed work. Also called a finished rough, it may consist of drawings, typeset copy, photographically produced prints, or a combination of such elements.

PRESS RELEASE Specially written information supplied to the media together with photographs related to a client's products.

PRIMARY COLOURS Pure colours from which all other colours can be mixed. In subtractive colour mixing, used in printing, they are magenta, cyan and yellow. The primary colours of light, or additive colours, are red, blue and green.

PRINT RUN The number of copies required from a printer and the process of printing the copies.

PRINTOUT (1) A general term for the record of information made by a printing device attached to a computer. (2) An enlarged copy made from a microform.

PROCESS CAMERA A camera designed for process work in photomechanical reproduction techniques.

PROCESS COLOURS The four colours of printing inks – cyan, magenta, yellow and black.

PROCESS WHITE An opaque white gouache for correction and masking of artwork intended for reproduction.

PROGRESSIVE PROOFS The proofs taken in colour printing as a guide to shade and registration. Each colour is shown separately and also imposed on the preceding colour.

PROMOTION Presentation and advertising intended to encourage the production and marketing of a product.

PROOF An impression obtained from an inked plate, stone, screen, block or type in order to check the progress and accuracy of the work. It is also called a pull.

PROOF CORRECTION MARKS A standard set of signs and symbols commonly understood by all those involved in preparing copy for publication.

PROOF READER A person who reads proofs to correct and revise copy where necessary.

PROOFING PRESS A press, sometimes hand-operated, usually smaller than that used in the full print run, on which copy is proofed.

PULP The basic material used in papermaking, broken down chemically or mechanically.

PUT TO BED The state of printing plates or formes when they are secured to the press ready to print.

Q

QUAD Four times the normal paper size – 35 × 45 in (890 × 143 mm).

R

R-TYPE A direct process of producing photographic colour prints, developed by Kodak, R19 is the production of a print from artwork R1q4 from a transparency.

RAGGED LEFT/RIGHT Typeset copy in which the lines of type are not aligned at left/right.

RANGED LEFT/RIGHT A form of setting in which lines of unequal length form a vertical either on the lefthand side of the column or on the right.

RAPIDOGRAPH Brand of technical pens.

REAM 500 sheets of paper.

REGISTER MARKS The crosses, triangles and other devices used to position paper or film correctly.

RETAINER A fee paid to a designer or consultant by a client to retain his/her availability, not a fee for work carried out.

RETOUCHING Methods of altering the image in artwork or photography, to make corrections, improve or change the character of the image.

REVERSE B TO W Reverse black to white. An instruction to the printer to reverse the tones of an image.

REVERSE OUT An image that appears white out of a solid background, usually produced by photomechanical techniques.

RING BINDER A mechanical binding device in which leaves are secured through punched holes by means of metal rings.

RIVERS The streaks of white spacing produced when spaces in consecutive lines of type coincide.

ROMAN Ordinary vertical type as distinct from italic.

ROMAN NUMERALS A system of numerical notation based on the symbols I (one), V (five), X (10), L (50), C (100), D (500) and M (1000), used in combinations to represent any figure.

ROTARY PRESS A web-fed newspaper press which uses a cylindrical printing surface. The papers are delivered folded and counted, ready to be dispatched.

ROUGH An initial sketch representing a proposed design or idea.

RUB-ONS (US) A colloquial term for dry transfer lettering.

RULES Metal strips, of type height, in various widths and lengths, used for printing lines. It is also a term for lines generally.

RULING PEN A pen used to draw lines of constant width. The ink or paint is held between two metal fingers.

RUN ON Instruction to printer that the text is continuous and no new paragraph is to be made.

RUNNING HEAD The line of type which repeats a chapter heading etc at the top of a page.

RUNNING TEXT A body of text which runs over from one page to another even when there are breaks for illustrations and diagrams.

RUN-ROUND TEXT Type that is laid out to follow the outline shape of an illustration.

S

SADDLE-STITCH/WIRE A method of stitching brochures: they are opened over a saddle-shaped support and stitched through the back.

SANS SERIF A typeface without serifs and usually without stroke contrast.

SCALING, SCALING UP Determining the degree of enlargement or reduction necessary to reproduce an original image within a given area of a design. The scaling may be represented as a percentage of the image area or in figures proportional to the dimensions of the original.

SCAMP A rough sketch showing the basic idea for an advertisement or design.

SCANNER A device used in photomechanical reproductions to identify electronically the density of colours in an image for colour separation.

SCATTER PROOFS Proofs for checking the quality of illustrations in photomechanical reproduction. To reduce proofing costs, as many images as possible are proofed altogether, with no reference to correct positions in a layout.

SCHEMATIC A drawing or diagram showing the components and procedures of a particular activity or system.

SCORE To make a crease in paper or card so that it it will not be damaged by folding.

SCRAPERBOARD/SCRATCHBOARD (UK/US) A prepared board with a gesso surface. First it is inked and then scraped or scratched with a point or blade to give the effect of a white line engraving.

SCREEN ANGLE The angle at which a halftone screen is arranged in the process of connecting continuous tone colour separations to screened film. Each separation unit be screened at a particular angle to avoid a moiré pattern.

SCREEN CLASH A disruptive pattern in an image produced when two or more halftone screens have been positioned at incorrect angles.

SCREEN PRINTING Printing method in which ink is forced through the fine mesh of a fabric or metal screen. The image is formed by a stencil made photographically on the screen or a cut stencil that adheres to the screen

SCRIPT A typeface designed to imitate handwriting.

SECONDARY COLOURS Colours obtained when two primary colours are mixed.

SECTION (1) A sheet folded to create four or more book pages.

SELF ENDS Endpapers formed from a leaf from the first section at the front, and the last section at the back of a book.

SEPARATION ARTWORK Artwork in which a separate layer is created for each colour to be printed, usually by means of translucent overlays.

SEPIA TONING A method of changing black and white photographic prints to sepia (brown) tones with chemical bleach and dye.

SERIF The small terminal stroke at the end of the main stroke of a letter.

SET (1) The width of a type body. (2) It is used as an instruction as in 'set to 12 picas' or as a description, ie, 'handset'. (3) It has a special sense to describe the proportions of the em of a size and type.

SET CLOSE Describes type set with the minimum of space between the words and no extra space between the sentences.

SET OFF (1) The accidental transference of an image from one printed sheet to the back of the next impression. (2) An impression taken from a key outline of a design which is powdered with a non-greasy dye while the ink is damp, then placed on the stone or plate and passed through the press.

SET SOLID Setting in which the line spacing is the same size as the type, eg 9/9pt is 9pt solid.

SET-SQUARE (UK) Drawing aid in the form of a flat plastic or metal right-angled triangle.

SHEET A single piece of paper or board.

SHOOT A photographic session.

SHOW THROUGH The fault in which a printed impression on one side of the paper is visible on the other side through the paper.

SHRINK WRAPPING Thin, transparent plastic film used in packaging. It is sealed tight around an object by heat action.

SIDE-STAB/STITCH A method of securing the sections of a book, with wires passed through close to the back.

SIGNATURE The letter at the tail of the first page of each section in a book, running in alphabetical order, which serves as a guide to the binder in gathering.

SILK SCREEN PRINTING Screen printing using a screen made of silk, the traditional method often still used in printing fine art editions.

SINGLE LENS REFLEX A rollfilm camera in which the image seen in the viewfinder and that recorded on the film are transmitted through the same lens.

SIXTEEN SHEET A standard poster size measuring 120 × 80 in (3050 × 2030 mm).

SIZE A gelatinous solution used to coat paper, to glaze or seal the surface and render the paper less porous. Size may be based on glue, casein, starch or a similar substance.

SLAB SERIFS Square serifs of almost the same thickness as the uprights, used in most Egyptian typefaces.

SLIP CASE An open-sided case to hold one or more books, with their spines showing.

SLOPED ROMAN A typeface commonly termed italic but actually a sloping version of Roman type.

SMALL CAPITALS Captials letters which are smaller than the standard and usually aligned with the ordinary line of type. They are indicated by a double underlining in manuscript.

SMALL FACE The smaller version of a typeface cast in two sizes on one body.

SOFT COPY (1) The copy displayed to the keyboard operator on a viewing screen. (2) (US) Typed copy used for checking a text before camera ready copy is produced.

SOFT EDGE Outlines of an image that are not clearly defined.

SOFT FOCUS A photographic effect in which the image is slightly diffused to soften the lines and edges of a shape without distorting the true focus. There are different ways of achieving the effect, such as with a specially made filter or shooting through a glass plate smeared with petroleum jelly.

SOFTWARE A term used for computer programs and general items. It also refers to paper and magnetic tape.

SOLID The backbone of a publication that encloses and secures the back edges of the paper in binding.

SPECIFICATION, SPEC A description of the components, characteristics and procedures of a particular job, product or activity.

SPIRAL BINDER A spiral wire holding the leaves of a book together.

SPOILS, BOOTY, SPOILAGE Badly printed sheets which are discarded before delivery of a job.

SPOTTING Retouching of photographic prints to cover tiny spots and blemishes affecting the image.

SPRAY The fine mist of air and paint expelled from an airbrush.

SPREAD Two facing pages of a publication.

SQUARED UP HALFTONE A halftone image confined to a rectangular shape.

SRA PAPER SIZES The description of untrimmed paper in the series of international paper sizes.

SAME SIZE, S/S An instruction to the printer to reproduce an image at the same size as the original.

STET A Latin word meaning 'let it stand'. It is used in proof correcting to cancel a previously marked correction.

STIPPLE A mechanical method of obtaining a background which could not be achieved by hand in the original. These areas are indicated by blue shading on the original.

STOP OUT A chemical treatment for printing plates that removes any unwanted copy or marks.

STORYBOARD A series of illustrations, rather like a comic strip, which represent a sequence of events that will eventually be filmed.

STRAPLINE A secondary heading to a newspaper or magazine story, amplifying the main heading.

STRIPPING Two or more photographic images assembled to produce a composite image.

SUB-HEADS Minor headlines that are used to divide copy into separate items on a printed page.

SWASH CHARACTERS Old face italic types with calligraphic flourishes.

SWATCH A colour specimen supplied to the printer to which the ink can be matched.

SYMBOL A letter, figure or drawn sign that represents or identifies an object, process or activity.

SYNOPSIS A condensed version of the thesis and contents of a book, giving a clear breakdown of the likely or actual progression of the text.

T

TABLOID A page half the size of broadsheet.

TEAR SHEET An image, feature or advertisement torn from a periodical and filed as reference material.

TECHNICAL ILLUSTRATION A highly-finished illustration designed to show mechanical objects or systems in a totally accurate and realistic manner.

TECHNICAL PEN A pen with a tubular nib designed to draw lines of an even width.

TEXT The written or printed matter forming the main body of a publication.

THICK The description of a word space used in hand-set type measuring 1/3 of an em.

THIN A word space as above measuring 1/5 of an em.

THIRTY TWO SHEET A poster size measuring 120 × 160 in (3040 × 4060 mm).

THREE-DIMENSIONAL (3-D) (1) An image creating the illusion of standing out physically from the page. (2) An object, such as a package, which has depth as well as height and width.

THUMBNAIL SKETCHES Small rough sketches used to work out an idea.

TINT (1) The effect of the admixture of white to a solid colour. (2) The effect achieved by breaking up colour into a percentage using dots which allow white paper to show through.

TIP IN/ON An illustration printed on a single page and inserted separately in a book, by pasting one edge.

TITLE PAGE The righthand page at the front of a book which bears the title, the names of author and publisher, the place of publication and other relevant information.

TITLE VERSO The page following the title page of a book.

TITLING A headline type, always in capitals.

TONAL VALUE The relative densities of tones in an image.

TONE The variations of shade in one colour.

TRANNY Transparency.

TRANSFER A film or acetate sheet bearing an image for transfer to a printing plate.

TRANSFER LETTERING Preprinted lettering or other images stored on a transparent sheet or cellulose acetate. Dry lettering is transferred to paper or artboard by burnishing the shape from the front of the sheet. Wet transfers are applied using water.

TRANSPARENCY A photographically developed image on transparent film. The term usually refers to a positive image in colour, though it is also applicable to any image on a transparent base.

TRANSPOSE To change the order of characters, words, lines or images on a manuscript or proof.

TRIM MARKS Marks incorporated in a printed sheet to indicate where paper stock is to be trimmed or cut to size.

TWICE UP Artwork or copy prepared at twice the size at which it will be reproduced.

TYPE, TYPEFACE The raised image of a character cast on a rectangular piece of metal used in letterpress printing.

TYPE FAMILY A term covering all the variations and sizes of a basic typeface design.

TYPE MARK-UP Instructions marked on copy to be printed giving the compositor details of point size, typeface etc.

TYPE SCALE/GAUGE A rule marked with a scale of type measurements, points, ems, picas etc, used by designers and compositors.

TYPESETTING Methods of assembling type for printing, by hand, machine or photographic technique.

TYPOGRAPHY The art and process of arranging type.

U

UNIVERSAL COPYRIGHT CONVENTION An international agreement dating from 1952 agreed to protect the originator of a design or illustration against his material being reproduced without permission. The work must carry the copyright mark © and the name of the individual or organization which holds the copyright as well as the date of publication.

UNJUSTIFIED Lines of type which are centred or which align only at one margin and are not adjusted in spacing to fill out the full measure of the line.

UPPER CASE The capital letters in a fount of typeface.

V

VACUUM FORMING A method of shaping plastic sheet by heating it until it softens before it is pulled down over a relief mould by the vacuum created beneath the mould.

VDU/VDT VISUAL DISPLAY UNIT/VISUAL DISPLAY TERMINAL A device for displaying information forming the input or output of a computer operated system.

VELLUM The treated skin of a calf, kid or lamb, used as a writing surface.

VERSO The lefthand page of a book.

VIDEO Videotape recording. Literally television but more commonly refers to a method of recording visual images on tape with sound, with a facility for viewing the recording as it is being made. The image monitor is a television set.

VIGNETTE A small illustration or decoration without a border.

VIGNETTED HALFTONE A halftone image in which tones gradually bleed out into the background.

VISUAL A mock-up of the proposed appearance of a design or layout presented as a rough drawing, or if more highly finished, as a presentation visual.

VISUALIZE To translate an initial idea into graphic terms by way of illustration.

W

WATERMARK A distinctive design incorporated in paper during manufacture.

WEB A continuous roll of paper.

WEB-SET An offset press working from a web or reel of paper.

WIDOW A single word standing as the last line of a paragraph in typeset copy.

WIRE BINDING Method of mechanical binding where slots are drilled through the cover and pages, then secured with ringed wire fingers. Also known as 'wiro'.

WIRE STITCH/STAB One of a line of wire staples passed through the back of a printed section used as a method of binding.

WOODCUT A relief printing method using the side grain of a wood block. Areas not intended to print are cut away below the surface of the block leaving a raised image that can be inked.

WORD PROCESSOR Equipment usually interfaced with a computer, so that input copy can be stored and automatically printed out at high speed, so the stored information can be quickly corrected or revised.

WORD SPACING The adjustment of space between words in copy being set, using fixed or variable space widths according to the method of composition.

WORK AND TUMBLE To print one side of a sheet and turn it from front to back to print the second side, keeping the same alignment of the side edges on the press.

WORK AND TURN When matter for both sides of a sheet is set in one forme. After one side of the sheet has been printed it is turned over end for end and backed up from the same forme.

WORK AND TWIST To print the same forme twice on the same side of a sheet, turning the sheet through 90° between printings.

WORK UP To keep developing an initial sketch until the desired effect is achieved.

X

X-HEIGHT The height of letters with neither ascenders or descenders eg 'x'.

INDEX